UNT DUVET OF DARKNESS

VOLUME TWO
LURKING MERKINS

POEMS WRITTEN BY ANGRY WOMEN FOR ANGRY WOMEN

BECAUSE

WOMEN WON'T WHEESHT

Edited by Boiledbeetle

© This collection: Boiledbeetle 2023

All rights reserved

ISBN: 9798865025016

No part of this publication may be reproduced, distributed, or transmitted in any form or by any means, including photocopying, recording, or other electronic or mechanical methods, without the prior written permission of the copyright owner, except as permitted by UK copyright law.

October 2023

For

Elaine and her merkin

CONTENTS

FOREWORD		13
COPYRIGHT ACKNOWLEDGEMENTS		14
ACKNOWLEDGEMENTS		15
INTRODUCTION		17
CHAPTER 1: LETTER TO MY DAUGHTER		19
1	The four magic words	21
2	The sparking path	23
3	What is a woman?	24
4	Woman	25
5	A beautiful mess	25
6	Bonus	26
7	On being female	26
8	What's it called?	27
9	Watchful waiting	28
10	You told me you were trans	29
11	Kisses XX	32
12	Done playing	33
13	The word is woman	33
CHAPTER 2: WOMEN WON'T WHEESHT		35
14	Duthie Park	37
15	Ragin'	38
16	Law and order	38
17	Criminal behaviour	39
18	The lowlifes of Duthie Park	39
19	I wint tae dunce tae Abba	40
20	Women Won't Wheesht	41
CHAPTER 3: THE GREAT GASLIGHTING ERA		45
21	Shall I compare thee to a TRA?	47
22	They	48
23	A misogynist's wet dream	49
24	Lurking	50
25	Peakers	50
26	Something for the weekend…	51

CHAPTER 3: THE GREAT GASLIGHTING ERA continued

27	Narcissistic entitlement	51
28	End of the world	52
29	The basement boys	53
30	The Met	54
31	Best laid plans	54
32	Not all women are equal	55
33	Update	56
34	Bobblehead	58
35	Final curtain	58
36	The beginning of the end of gender ideology	59
37	Bragging rights	59
38	The bluffer	60
39	Cuckoo	62

CHAPTER 4: GO FORTH AND CLENCH 63

40	Middle of the night	65
41	EHRC	66
42	Let's play	67
43	Spread eagled	67
44	Little Miss	68
45	Taking the piss	69

CHAPTER 5: WHEN THEE BUILDS A PRISON 71

46	#SSSAOR	73
47	No	74
48	This old man	75
49	Fear	76
50	A cockerel in the hen house	77
51	We've had enough	78

CHAPTER 6: FEMINIST TO MY FINGERTIPS 79

52	Wee keek	81
53	Wheesht woman	82
54	Great expectations	82
55	Exit stage left	82
56	Exit stage right	83
57	Trap door opens	83
58	Curtain closes	83
59	The holiday	84
60	The winter's tempest	85

CHAPTER 6: FEMINIST TO MY FINGERTIPS continued

61	Wasnae me	86
62	Go for it	87
63	Come on	88
64	What's in a name?	89
65	Oh Nicola!	90
66	Things left unsaid	90
67	The verdict	91

CHAPTER 7: GANNETS EVERY ONE OF THEM   93

68	Sweet dreams	95
69	Addicted	95
70	Tunnock's sisters	96
71	T Tunnock Ltd	97
72	A quick byte	99

CHAPTER 8: THE FAILURE OF COERCION   101

73	The Merkin Lady	103
74	Puppet on a string	105
75	The undoing	106
76	Equality and human rights	108
77	Taking Stock	109
78	Pride or shame	111
79	Uncharitable	112
80	You'll have had your Enlightenment then?	113
81	DIY	114
82	A non-ordinary woman	115
83	Song of the Mumsnetters	116
84	Genderwocky	117
85	The interview	118
86	Keir	119
87	Transformation	120
88	Hit Parade	121
89	The Honourable Lady	122
90	Humza	123

CHAPTER 9: WOMAN'S CYCLE   125

91	Balls	127
92	The cycle of life	128
93	Dai's bell	129

CHAPTER 10: WHY WE OPPOSE POCKETS FOR WOMEN — 131

94	Pockets of discontent	133
95	Stuff	134
96	Is that a beetle?	135
97	Put some effort in	135
98	Pocket rocket	136
99	Many	136

CHAPTER 11: UNDER THE DUVET OF DARKNESS — 137

100	Last orders	140
101	Bad Poets Society	140
102	Thank you	141
103	Lola	142
104	200	143
105	Interrupted	143
106	The book review	144
107	Amazing	145
108	Volume two	145
109	What would Magdalen say?	146
110	Under the Duvet of Darkness	147
111	Dress up	148
112	Wood	148
113	Ova	148
114	Tunnock's and poems	148
115	Prick up your ears	149
116	Pop	150
117	Goal!	150
118	Boiling point	150

CHAPTER 12: I'M NOT A VET BUT I KNOW WHAT A DOG IS — 151

119	Billy goat's bluff	153
120	Of cats and men and litter trays	154
121	Cats (and not-cats)	155
122	Cool as cats	156
123	Tiddles	157
124	Fly birdie fly	157
125	Wolf in sheep's clothing	158
126	Here kitty kitty	159

CHAPTER 13: FOOLISH MEN — 161

127	A ladyman's song	163
128	For Pete's sake	165
129	Plum gig	165
130	Decision time	166

CHAPTER 13: FOOLISH MEN continued

131	Closing arguments	168
132	Truth	168
133	That's enough	169
134	Incorrect	169
135	Born this way	170
136	Antithesis	171
137	Can people change sex?	172
138	Joining the dots	172
139	The wankerchief	173
140	An ode to the cervix grower	173

CHAPTER 14: SHE IS 14... SHE'S AWESOME — 175

141	Welcome to womanhood	177
142	Roll your skirt down	178
143	Top 10	179
144	Angst	180

CHAPTER 15: I'D RATHER BE RUDE THAN A FUCKING LIAR — 181

145	When the world went mad	183
146	I do not accept	184
147	Violation	185
148	Quids in	187
149	Know my place	188
150	Questions	189
151	My turn	190
152	Sick and tired	191
153	Enough now!	192
154	Keep fighting	193
155	Go forth and multiply	193
156	Silence	194
157	A tale as old as time	195
158	The dating game	199
169	Not a yes	200
160	Sturgeon approved court case	201
161	Inclusivity on platform 13	202

AFTERWORD — 205

ABBREVIATIONS — 206

ADDITIONAL INFORMATION — 207

FOREWORD

As with the first volume of Under the Duvet of Darkness 100% of the profit from the sale of this book* will be donated to For Women Scotland in honour of Magdalen Berns.

For Women Scotland are a group of women from all over Scotland. They work to protect and strengthen women and children's rights.

The group was founded in June 2018 due to unease about women's rights, and how they would be affected by the Scottish Government's plans to reform the Gender Recognition Act 2004 to allow for self-ID of sex.

For Women Scotland** do not receive any public money and are not aligned to any political party. All the staff are volunteers.

"How much longer are women going to stand for this insult?"

Magdalen Berns

(1983 – 2019)

*Please note that whilst the profit will be donated to For Women Scotland they are not involved, nor are they responsible in any way for the themes, contents or publication of this book.

**For Women Scotland has been registered as a not-for-profit company since July 2020 (Company number: SC669393). More information about For Women Scotland can be found at: https://forwomen.scot/

COPYRIGHT ACKNOWLEDGEMENTS

POEM COPYRIGHT HOLDERS

© AmaryllisNightAndDay Poem: 83
© AppleTreeOwner Poem: 69
© ArcaneWireless Poems: 6, 12, 15, 16, 17, 19, 42, 43, 44, 61, 62, 63, 74, 87, 91, 92,103, 104, 111, 116
© beastlyslumber Poem: 107
© Boiledbeetle Poems: 1, 4, 8, 11, 14, 25, 26, 32, 33, 39, 50, 65, 66, 67, 71, 73, 79, 82, 85, 88, 99, 100, 105, 106, 109, 120, 124, 126, 130, 131, 134, 146, 153, 155
© BonfireLady Poem: 10
© Bowednotbroken Poem: 49
© BreadInCaptivity Poem: 34
© Britinme Poem: 135
© Brokendaughter Poems: 2, 29, 48, 94, 101, 160
© Calyx72 Poem: 28
© CervixSampler Poems: 20, 68, 70, 112, 113, 114, 129, 136, 139, 157, 159
© Croneofakind Poem: 84
© CyclingSam Poem: 38
© FairyKindleMother Poems: 149, 156
© GingerbreadCookieDough Poems: 141, 142, 143, 144
© howdoesatoastermaketoast Poems: 3, 115, 127
© IcakethereforeIam Poems: 18, 88, 93, 95, 145
© LarkLane Poem: 37
© Larpingasapoet Poems: 46, 81, 128, 150
© lechiffre55 Poem: 83
© MissLucyEyelesbarrow Poem: 83
© Motorina Poem: 121
© MrInbetween Poem: 13
© Piccalillipromises Poems: 119, 125, 133
© PoembyChatGPT Poems: 72, 102
© PurpleBugz Poems: 147, 151
© Ramblingnamechanger Poem: 138
© RealFeminist Poems: 59, 64, 96
© Ritasueandbobtoo9 Poems: 9, 30, 41, 76, 77, 86, 122, 137, 154
© SaleOfTwoTitties Poems: 5, 110
© Somanyquestionstoaskaboutthis Poems: 132, 148
© SpottyBumPony Poem: 7
© Swashbuckled Poem: 161
© TessoftheDurbeyfields Poems: 53, 54, 55, 56, 57, 58, 89, 90, 98
© TheBiologyStupid Poems: 21, 60, 97, 108
© TheYorkshireTwat Poem: 158
© UrinaryLeash Poems: 31, 40, 45, 152
© Vebrithien Poems: 47, 51
© Waitwhat23 Poems: 23, 24, 27, 35, 36, 52, 78, 80, 117, 118, 123, 140
© Whatthechicken Poem: 75
© WinnieFosterFights Poem: 22

"I will bloody huff,
and puff! Your life?
Blown up into chaos!"
Wolf in grannie's dress!

The men now rule,
though, was ever so.
But this is now.
Two thousand twenty three.

This is not right.
We women must fight,
to keep men out
of all our spaces.

Men cannot just demand
things so not true.
We do not consent.
We will not relent

on these four words.
For they are ours,
and our words alone.
They belong to us,

not to a man.
Man has no right
to utter those words.
Only we can say:

"I AM A WOMAN"

Boiledbeetle 15th June 2023

1 THE FOUR MAGIC WORDS

"I am a woman!"
He pronounces to all.
And in that moment
the predator becomes prey.

The oppressor the oppressed.
Means that the man
holds all the aces.
Women only: now entered.

The women fall silent.
The man just gloats
at the glorious intrusion,
into female only places.

Rape group? Free entry.
Toilets? Come on in.
Prisons? Take your pick!
Changing room? There too.

These 'women' are men.
"Known since aged four."
Says the autogynephilic man.
That is not true.

Do not dare retort,
or even make waves.
If you say "NO!"
Then: hate crime report.

CHAPTER 1

LETTER TO MY DAUGHTER

Maya Angelou (1928-2014) was an American poet, memoirist, and civil rights activist. **'Letter to My Daughter'** is the title of a book of essays written by Maya. She had no daughters, so she wrote the book for all of the women who saw her as a mother figure. In her own words:

"Dear Daughter... I gave birth to one child, a son, but I have thousands of daughters... You are fat and thin and pretty and plain, gay and straight, educated and unlettered, and I am speaking to you all. Here is my offering to you."

With that in mind, where necessary I have included some 'enlightenment' after some poems to give the reader some contextual information about what triggered a poem to be written.

And finally, as you will have noticed this book is dedicated to the heroic merkin, and its wearer, who flashed itself to the world on 22nd December 2022. However, it was not alone. According to a reliable source there were 12 other merkins, ready to do their duty for their country, in Holyrood that day. Unfortunately, as the vote on the Gender Recognition Reform (Scotland) Bill had been moved from the 21st to the 22nd December 2022 Elaine Miller was left to flash her merkin alone.

At the end of that momentous day those 12 brave, but unused, merkins were tragically left behind in Holyrood. It turns out that being stuck behind a cubicle stall in the loos in Holyrood is fairly boring, so the merkins wrote poems. At some point one of them crept out of their hiding place and hid a poem from each of them within the pages of this book.

Happy reading, and merkin hunting! As always

WOMEN WON'T WHEESHT

Women of the Mumsnet FWR board October 2023

*Twitter: The poems in this book were written before and after Twitter changed its name to X. I don't fancy writing X (formerly known as Twitter) every time it crops up so it remains as Twitter and tweets throughout.

SMALL PRINT

To those who bought the e-book version of the first book, remember those bonus poems you got with the e-book? Well about that...

These books are about giving women, who are sometimes silenced in so many areas of their life, a voice. A chance to say what they need to say. So, it didn't seem right that those writers who agreed for their poems to go in the e-book version of the first book not get their poems read and enjoyed by the many people who bought the paperback version of the first one, and have hopefully bought Volume Two.

So, as this is a charitable endeavour, I hope you will understand if you happen to read a few poems that feel a little familiar.

INTRODUCTION

Hello! Here we are again. This is rather unexpected. Honestly, the first book was going to be a one off, but some of the women of Mumsnet's FWR (Feminism and Women's Rights) board would not stop writing poems. So, the only logical option was to do volume two. So many women had something they wished to say that it felt right that these poems should also be published for all to read as well.

Whilst we have come down, a smidgen, from the level of raging anger we felt over Christmas and the New year, it is safe to say we are still operating at a level of anger that makes for good poems! The anger and bleakness felt by many, after the passing of the GRR (Scotland) Bill, while we waited to see if the Secretary of State for Scotland would intervene, was thankfully lifted by Alister Jack when he issued the Section 35 Order in the middle of January 2023.

The Section 35 Judicial Review Substantive Hearing was held on Tuesday 19th and Wednesday 20th September 2023. The judge was Lady Haldane who will issue her judgement any time before the end of the year.

The poems contained within this book were written over 7 months (April through to October 2023), and cover a broad range of topics. There are poems about incidents that have occurred in regards to the issues surrounding trans rights coming into conflict with women's rights and gender critical beliefs. There are poems that show how some women feel in general about the whole thing, and then are some which hopefully offer much needed light relief.

The opening up of Twitter* to allow users with gender critical beliefs to speak more freely, without fear of being banned, alongside the stupidity and downright ludicrous behaviour of some on the trans rights side of history has forced the conversation further into the mainstream. 'No debate' has effectively had its day and those who previously shouted it are now expected, finally, to explain themselves. It will surprise no one reading this that they have been unable to. Instead, like an abusive husband who senses his wife is about to leave, the public fuckwittery of the TRAs just keeps ramping up a notch. There is definitely a poem or two about some of their more memorable moments!

Now that the wheels are, in all walks of life, finally beginning to fall off they's ;-) bus it seems a period of enlightenment is upon us, one in which the general public finally start to see, and hear about, what is happening.

ACKNOWLEDGEMENTS

All the poem writers in this book are grateful to Mumsnet who let us post our poems and thoughts on their FWR (Feminism and Women's Rights) board. We really do value the fact that Mumsnet provides us with a place where we are able to discuss what is currently happening to women in the name of 'inclusion' (although they still don't like us putting the words 'cock' and 'frock' in the same post).

The poems in this book were posted by over 40 different usernames. Thank you to all the posters who encouraged us with their comments and musings, they were very much appreciated.

I want to say a massive thank you on behalf of all the poem writers to the wonderful FairyKindleMother who has donated her skills and time for free to produce the e-book version of both volumes of Under the Duvet of Darkness. I really wish I could tell you who she actually is because she is bloody amazing!

I'm personally grateful to those posters who have kept me motivated whilst I put this book together. Their support and comments made the whole process a little less painful, even if some of the more evil ones kept posting more poems for me to incorporate!

I owe a huge debt of gratitude to Elaine Miller who on hearing of my merkin themed plans for this book didn't report me for stalking! So, Elaine, thank you for being the inspiration for many a poem written since 22nd December 2022. You have placed merkins firmly in the consciousness of the masses, but then that merkin was rather difficult to miss!

Finally, to all the poem writers who allowed me to use their words in this book thank you so much. Without you there would be no book. As always, I am eternally grateful.

Boiledbeetle xx

2 THE SPARKING PATH

There is a sparking path, where only women walk,
no matter what preventions are in place,
without regard for science saying so.
A furled up bud of hope, all women hold within,
entire civilisations of potential,
that only women know.

There is a rock strewn cliff, that only women climb,
to fall on the dual edged blade of grief/relief.
When blooded proof unfurls,
or bloodless pause insists,
denotes a gift, denies a dream, depicts a fear, demands a choice,
that only women make.

There is a storm wracked mountain, that only women scale,
rippling, tear shuddering peaks as life in full bloom prevails,
summits of pain that cannot be remembered in it's all.
Of ravines screaming to the edge of death,
or sometimes past that point, fate swept away,
as only women are.

There is a tumbled moorland, that only women trek,
mired in misogyny laced with lies,
revealed in the mists as women forge ahead.
Bitter, weed choked revelation that our equality is false,
which only women learn.

There is a roaring waterfall, then rapids only women navigate,
to forge from fecund to the other side.
Overblown petals now, our time is passed,
to spark new generations,
as only women can.

There is a placid lake, where only women sail,
sweet fading blossoms dressed with greying heads.
Smile lines or frowns carve flexing, fading arcs,
those fecund days of youth now past.
Angered, freed to defend those future sparks,
as only women fight.

On all these paths, we women pass each other by,
as time and circumstances lead us through trials and trails,
we travel up and down as time ticks by.
Weaving our ways as maiden, mother, crone,
until days take us all to the quiet eddies at lakes edge,
where only women sit.

And in the eddies, at the end where women meet,
as buds and blossoms treasured on the wind,
we scent the future with our passing tracks.
Become memories of the beings that began,
as only women may.

No man can ever tread the sparking paths.
They cannot know just
what a woman is,
or learn humility enough to ask.
They never feel the footing change in life.
The what of we remains beyond their grasp.

Brokendaughter 8th June 2023

3 WHAT IS A WOMAN?

A woman is just
a little girl who grew up.
Growing up is hard.

howdoesatoastermaketoast 5th October 2023

4 WOMAN

Woman is not a hobby,
it's not a feeling, nor a game.
Woman is not the way
you find your fortune, or your fame.
Woman is a state of being,
not something that we choose.
Woman is what we are born as,
and a word we'll never lose.

Boiledbeetle 18th June 2023

5 A BEAUTIFUL MESS

My limbs are long,
my limbs are short,
I have flat loafers on my feet.
It makes no difference which shoes I bought,
you can tell I'm a woman,
whenever we meet.

My hips are narrow,
my hips are wide,
trousers skirt or dress.
It makes no difference the patterns I tried,
you can tell I'm a woman,
a beautiful mess.

Don't call me haver,
Don't call me cis.
Aggression and shadow,
I'll never be this.
Cancel and argue,
I'll say what I see.
You are not a woman.
You'll never be me.

SaleOfTwoTitties 25th August 2023

6 BONUS

A fadge, a fanny, a minnie, a foof,
a clunge, a slit, a muff or a moof.
A lulu, a minge, a vag or a nuun,
a growler, a fairy, a Mary, poon-poon.

A front bum, a cunt, a flower, vagina,
a flutey, a chutey, or just plain auld Gynah.
There are plenty of words, you know it is true,
for your pipe or your hole, your fluff or your flue.

Be inclusive, be kind, you've heard that is best,
I agree to a point then am put to the test.
For today I have heard of a new little name,
it conquered, it saw, it came - what a shame.

A 'bonus hole' of all things! We thought it meant arse,
but it doesn't, and you know it is part of that farce.
I suppose it was coined by a prince amongst men,
for the women I know don't have one of them.

ArcaneWireless 30th June 2023

7 ON BEING FEMALE

I once felt a great big bubble.
Had a feeling it was gonna be trouble.
I felt it slide from the front to the back.
Attempting to leave at the top of the crack.
In the end it popped out of my own channel tunnel.

SpottyBumPony 13th August 2023

8 WHAT'S IT CALLED?

Do you have a fanny?
Or do you have a foof?
Do you call it cunt?
Or are you more aloof?

Do you use its Sunday name,
and call it a vagina?
Or maybe call it Coco,
after the designer.

If you are a woman
then you definitely have a vag.
There's no need to announce
it with a pronoun badge.

But if you are a man
and you think you too have one,
what you have is a bonus hole
made from penis or colon.

Boiledbeetle 26th August 2023

Enlightenment: poems 6 and 8

In June 2023 it came to light that Jo's Cervical Cancer Trust recommends the use of the term 'bonus hole' for vagina so as not to upset transgender people.

9 WATCHFUL WAITING

Under the duvet,
we watch and wait.

We see what's happening,
we watch and wait.

We see women lose,
we watch and wait.

We see women raped,
we watch and wait.

We see women silenced,
we watch and wait.

We see women mutilated,
we watch and wait.

Under the duvet.

Ritasueandbobtoo9 5th May 2023

10 YOU TOLD ME YOU WERE TRANS

You told me you were trans,
I said, that's OK.
What's the big deal?
It's just like being gay.

You told me you need blockers,
My gut said, just wait.
There's something deeper here;
the script then starts to play.

You're not sure you're a girl,
your body needs to change.
You're young but you're sure,
and it's not like being gay.

I listen and I learn,
I'm lost for what to say.
We find our path together, but
the world pulls us both one way.

The wrench you feel is real,
the boards you tread bring pain.
The more I learn, the more
I find a twisted modern game.

You're broken and you're hurting,
there's so much more in play.
The answer calls, with kindness
an answer to your pain.

I won't hold you back, but
I won't let you be swayed,
by the wave of love which pulls you in,
that's more than just a craze.

It's compelling, and it's trying
to get you in its gaze.
To tell you that the answer is
to trans the pain away.

We work through this together,
but I can never say
what I feel is right. If I push too hard
I'll push you far away.

Your path through life is yours alone,
but I'm here all the way,
to help you find your own true self,
it's more than just a game.

You told me you were trans,
but now you feel a change.
You don't know what comes next,
have you found the strength to wait?

BonfireLady 7th September 2023

Enlightenment: poem 10

A letter to my daughter,

My gorgeous 14-year-old girl, you'll see this poem when you're older and by then this particular difficult time in your life will be behind you. The world is a tough place. It's even tougher when you're autistic.

As your mum, my job isn't to tell you what choices you should make. It's to protect you from making choices now; when you're in distress and when social media, health professionals, and well-meaning adults are suggesting to you that changing your body irreversibly is the answer to all your problems.

Even asking you what pronouns you use, because you've got short hair and wear "boys' clothes", is asking you whether you're really happy with being a girl or if you might want to opt out of that.

My job is also to arm you with the critical thinking skills that you'll need to navigate life. I'm doing the best job that I can.

I'm also fighting hard, both anonymously and in person, to save others, just like you, from getting swallowed up in the biggest medical scandal of modern times.

I love you and always will.

Mum xx

11 KISSES XX

I never asked to be like this, but I was born this way.
How I wished for something different, day after bloody day.
I wanted things I couldn't have, but no matter how I wished,
still every day I'd wake up to find I'm still like this.
The dresses, and the dolls, I hated with a passion.
Dungarees, and wellie boots, were much much more my fashion.

As an adult I could choose how I wished to live my life,
so I made the right decision, I'd be no mother, nor a wife.
I'd live the life I wanted, and wear whatever I like.
I'd go into construction, and yes, get called a dyke.
In time I made my peace with the sex I had been born.
Thank God I'm not a child now, cos I would be so torn.

The teachers they would tell me I should have been a boy,
just because I hated skirts, and played with the wrong toy.
They'd pass me onto therapists, who'd affirm that I was right.
They'd tell me that my breasts could be bound all flat and tight.
The doctors would agree, and then fill me full of pills,
persuaded that's the right course by the Pharma corporate shills.

Then finally the surgeon, who'd sworn to do no harm.
I'd get my breasts removed; make a penis from my arm.
All to live the life I wanted, and to wear just what I like.
I would still have been a builder, and still got called a dyke.
You are what you are born as, there is no changing sex.
It's as it always has been, men are XY, and women XX.

Boiledbeetle 15th September 2023

12 DONE PLAYING

As a non-male can I say
I have no wish to bloody play
the games that you insist upon.
Know that we are fucking done.

So you want a manly world?
Get your penis flag unfurled.
Carry on with your daft caper.
Headline every bastard paper.

Cross your t's and get i-dotting.
Know that all your sinister plotting
will come to zero, zilch and nowt.
Still we rise. Be of no doubt.

"Be kind to all" is often touted.
"Not to women though" is shouted.
Loud and hard we hear you fine.
Today is yours. Tomorrow's MINE.

ArcaneWireless 24th September 2023

13 THE WORD IS WOMAN

So, I'm no longer a woman, I am a non-man.
My daughter is no longer a girl, but a non-boy.
My female hound is a non-dog.
My aunt is a non-uncle.
My sister is my non-brother.

And the world has finally lost the fucking plot.

MrInbetween 24th September 2023

CHAPTER 2

WOMEN WON'T WHEESHT

'Women Won't Wheesht' was coined by WitchCrit (@Dis_Critic) on 31st July 2020.

In response to a For Women Scotland tweet, about the redefinition of 'woman' in the Gender Representation on Public Boards (Scotland) Act 2018, WitchCrit (@Dis_Critic) replied with:

> "Thank you for this. I'm still in shock the country in which I live has seen fit to redefine woman for the purposes of any damn thing. This has been allowed to happen precisely because women never have been seen as equals. But they have a fight on their hands: **Women Won't Wheesht**."

14 DUTHIE PARK

PARTY IN DUTHIE PARK
1PM 23ʳᴅ JULY 2023
SEE BELOW FOR DETAILS

Duthie Park is where it's at,
no need to bring your baseball bat.

There will be singing, and dancing,
while on women we're advancing.

So mask up tight
and be ready to fight.

The women will provide the props
that you can use to assault the sops.

Your fist is good, but their banner is better.
You will get away with it. Honest! I bet yer!

You'll probably just get a slap on the wrist!
And those uppity women? God! They'll be pissed.

You see the Scottish Police are all MRAs,
they'll be doing the bidding of us TRAs.

So come to the 'Party in Duthie Park',
because punching women is such a lark!

Boiledbeetle 5th October 2023

15 RAGIN'

Wheesht o' the wimmin in the park
fan ane' o' the chiels took the nark.
He grabbed at her banner,
decided to tan her,
the intention wiz there and wiz stark.

But the thing aboot those fae oor toon
is we winnae be seen lyin' doon.
Tae them that's sae tough,
we've a' had enough,
know the granite is ours - silly loon.

For them that think muscley flexes
can convince us all o' yer new sexes,
I've got news ya prince,
yer heid's full o' mince,
for us wimmin are made wi twa X's.

ArcaneWireless 24th July 2023

16 LAW AND ORDER

A slap on the wrist? Min ye're funnin',
a chiel hittin' wimmin needs shunnin'.
The law needs re-settin'.
The impression ah'm gettin'
is that this man just ain't brave and
stunnin'.

ArcaneWireless 24th July 2023

17 CRIMINAL BEHAVIOUR

When you double down and see no ill,
when the tale of assault gathers pace,
just know we won't swallow your bitter pill,
you don't choose to stop fists with your face.

ArcaneWireless 25th July 2023

BEWARE

Beware the lurking merkin,
it will catch you unaware.
It will put the willies up you,
and give you quite a scare.

They lurk in Holyrood's lavs,
been there since last year!
So, if you fancy a memento
try and catch one if you dare!

LurkingMerkin No. 4

18 THE LOWLIFES OF DUTHIE PARK

(Inspired by 'The Fields of Athenry' by Pete St. John)

Lowlifes are free in Duthie Park,
where once we came to hear women speak.
Our rights are up for grabs,
here they come, all the lads.
There's no justice for females in Duthie Park.

IcakethereforeIam 24th September 2023

19 I WINT TAE DUNCE TAE ABBA

When some fowk in a toonser park
shout "Wumman ken yer place.
Ah've mair rights tae a skirt than ye,
so shut yer bastart face.

I wint tae dunce tae Abba,
an' yer spoilin' ma day oot.
Pit doon yer fuckin' banner,
I can slap yer teeth clean oot."

They ken they winnae be punished,
jist telt aff an' punted hame.
They cannae help their sharny sels,
they wint their chunce o' fame.

Dance an' pout an' cairry on,
we a' see whit ye're daein'.
Admit yer jist oot for the menz,
perhaps ye'll find it freein'.

Cairry on disrupting quines,
wi yer chunts an' singin'.
Dress it up in satin drawers,
we ken its baws yer swingin'.

ArcaneWireless 24th September 2023

20 WOMEN WON'T WHEESHT

I can't express the horror
of seeing where we are.
Our grandmothers, and great grandmothers,
will be turning in their graves.
They fought so hard for what they won,
what was theirs, and then ours.
Here we are fighting again, for what was already won,
but taken away by their sons, and grandsons.
We will fight, as one,
for our sisters north of the border.
We will stand, and stand as one.
Their fight is ours.
We won't stand down.
We won't stop fighting.
We won't stop striving.
We won't stop campaigning.
We won't stop marching.
We won't stop doing whatever we can.

Because **WOMEN WON'T WHEESHT!**

CervixSampler 24th September 2023

Enlightenment: poems 14 to 20

On 23rd July 2023 a group of women were gathered in Aberdeen's Duthie Park. Their intention was to speak to other women about being a woman, and all that entails. The thugs however were not happy. They had decided that women (a quarter of the way through the 21st century) should not be allowed to speak openly, and freely, about womanly things. And so, as now happens at many events held by women for women, a group of TRAs turned up to attempt to drown out the women's voices, and intimidate the women into silence.

One of the TRAs decided to steal a banner belonging to the campaign group 'Women Won't Wheesht'. Julie Marshall, one of the founders of Women Won't Wheesht, asked the man to give it back. The man's response to Julie's request was to assault her. He swung round and, holding the stolen banner in both hands, smashed Julie in the face with the banner using such force that her glasses were knocked off her face. She was also punched in the arm.

Such was the police concern for the woman who had just been assaulted that when the police turned up they went to the TRAs first. Then proceeded to speak with them for a full 10 minutes before going over to the group of women to check on Julie.

Tweeting about the event later Julie (@DarcyWAHF) said she was:

"Very shaken up will have a badly bruised arm and black eye. I'm definitely not gonna wheesht. They can beat us, and they can scream at us and call us names. But it only hardens our resolve. If you resort to violence, you have already lost."

On 24th July 2023 Women Won't Wheesht (@WWWheesht) tweeted:

"Make no mistake, we will NOT be silenced. We will NEVER stop speaking up for women's rights and we will NEVER stop hosting events to give women the opportunity to speak about their experiences and concerns. YOU WILL NOT BULLY US INTO SILENCE. YOUR VIOLENCE WILL NOT INTIMIDATE US. YOUR AGGRESSION MAKES US STRONGER. WOMEN WILL NEVER WHEESHT"

A Police Scotland spokesperson later said:

"On Sunday 23rd July 2023 officers were in attendance during an organised protest in the Duthie Park area of Aberdeen. We were made aware of an assault of a 54-year-old woman during the event and an individual, aged 26, has received a Recorded Police Warning in connection with the incident. There were no reports of any injuries and the protest later ended with no further issues."

Not that they actually bothered to contact Julie and tell her any of that before giving a statement to a local newspaper.

On 26th July 2023 the Edinburgh-based policy analysis collective Murray Blackburn Mackenzie wrote to the Chief Constable of Police Scotland, Iain Livingstone. In their letter to the police, Murray Blackburn Mackenzie pointed out that:

"Section 6 of the Human Rights Act 1998 states that 'It is unlawful for a public authority to act in a way which is incompatible with a Convention right'. Article 10 of the European Convention of Human Rights protects freedom of expression. Article 11 includes protection for freedom of peaceful assembly. We note that the Equalities and Human Rights Commission states that the Act requires all public bodies (like courts, police, local authorities, hospitals and publicly funded schools) and other bodies carrying out public functions to respect and protect your human rights.

How seriously the police take incidents of assault and attempted assault on women meeting peacefully to express certain lawful views will affect whether their rights under Articles 10 and 11 can be safely exercised in practice. We would therefore be grateful to know whether Police Scotland made any assessment of its obligations under the Human Rights Act 1998, before deciding how to treat this incident?"

In response a spokesperson for Police Scotland stated:

"As a result of an allegation of assault at the WWW rally on Sunday, a male suspect was identified and received a Recorded Police Warning, which is in line with the Lord Advocate's guidelines."

On 28th July 2023 Murray Blackburn Mackenzie wrote to the Lord Advocate, Rt Hon Dorothy Bain KC, to ask whether she agreed with Police Scotland that the action in this case was in line with guidelines issued on her behalf. Murray Blackburn Mackenzie asked that the guidelines be reviewed and amended, to ensure that they give proper weight to the responsibility of Police Scotland to protect ECHR rights under Articles 10 and 11.

On 29th August 2023 they received a response from the Procurator Fiscal that *"set some context to the Recorded Police warning (RPW) Scheme."*

A very detailed report by Murray Blackburn Mackenzie of the Recorded Police Warning Scheme and the need for transparency and accountability can be found at:

https://murrayblackburnmackenzie.org/2023/09/10/recorded-police-warnings-the-need-for-transparency-and-accountability/

The Lord Advocate's guidelines, which direct police officers on the scope of RPWs, remain confidential. Police Scotland has recently stated that it is looking to expand the RPW scheme.

CHAPTER 3

THE GREAT GASLIGHTING ERA

Sall Grover is the founder and CEO of 'giggle' a female social network. Sall is being taken to Federal Court in Australia for saying no to males in the female only space she created.

On 28th September 2023, Sall Grover (@salltweets) tweeted:

*"This period of history will be known as **The Great Gaslighting Era**."*

21 SHALL I COMPARE THEE TO A TRA?

(Inspired by 'Sonnet 18' by William Shakespeare)

Shall I compare thee to a TRA?
Thou art more lovely, and more gentle too.
Rough hands do shake the sharpened tools of hate,
and mental health is all destroyed by woo.
Sometime too obvious the penis of 'her' shows,
and often is that 'female' organ hymned.
And every option of fair sport declines,
not chance, but male biology, untrimmed.
But thy eventual victory shall prevail,
you'll keep possession of those rights thou ow'st.
Nor shall men brag they wander'st in thy jail,
when sanity at last begins to grow'st.
So long as women breathe and eyes can see,
so long lives sex, and thus reality.

TheBiologyStupid 13th April 2023

22 THEY

They said they were inclusive,
then pushed the women out.
They denied they dealt in stereotypes,
then began to pose and pout.

They said they were the victims,
then posed with guns and bats.
They ignored the deaths of women,
they cared not a jot for that.

They did care if women gathered,
if they met or tried to speak.
They'd shout and scream all over them,
leading many more to peak.

A woman's voice became the
worst thing you could hear.
It might say the emperor's naked,
and that was their biggest fear.

Their house of sticks was flimsy,
the truth could blow it all.
But the women, they were circling,
and they knew they'd make it fall.

WinnieFosterFights 10th April 2023

23 A MISOGYNIST'S WET DREAM

Men,
who masked for such a short while as 'good guys'
now have free rein.

Unleashed, they say all they wanted to but couldn't.
Bitch, witch, ugly, old. Bigot, TERF, frigid, cold.

Sheer orgasmic pleasure at 'telling those bitches'
whilst society cheers them on.

'DECAPITATE TERFS' above a smirk.
Screaming "WITCH" from above.
Forced smiles on a podium.

It was always there. Under the surface.
Seething, but contained.

But now? They can say, self-righteously,

"BURN THE WITCH!"

It's as it ever was.

Waitwhat23 28th May 2023

24 LURKING

'For the lurkers.'
A phrase given so much meaning,
due to the evidenced adept reasoning
of the posters of FWR.

Waitwhat23 19th June 2023

Enlightenment: poem 24

We know women read the FWR threads for a long time before posting. We know this because that's what most of us did when we first found the board. So, whilst to some it seems like a good idea to ignore the TRA who turns up on a thread looking for a fight, someone always takes them on. It helps to show the 'lurkers' the contradictions, lies and sometimes total batshittery of what the TRAs are posting.

25 PEAKERS

(Inspired by 'The Scarlet Pimpernel' by Baroness Emma Orczy)
(Oh, and by Waitwhat23's comment below!)

They peak them here; they peak them there.
Those TRA's peak them everywhere.
Are they from heaven, or are they from hell?
Those damned persistent infidels.

Boiledbeetle 19th June 2023

Enlightenment: poem 25

Comment by Waitwhat23: *"I want to put forward a thanks to all our frequent flyers, for their ongoing work towards peaking women. You are being told that you are directly peaking women and still you continue. I'm wondering whether we should start referring to you as 'peakers', in a similar way that people refer to allies etc. Thank you peakers! Carry on with the good work."*

26 SOMETHING FOR THE WEEKEND...

TRA here:

You bloody GC women, you are so bloody rude!
When I try to berate you, you just start to talk of food.

When I throw a strop, because you say 'lesbians don't do dick',
you begin to talk of Tunnock's, and which product you would pick.

When I try, repeatedly, to tell you that those men are actually she's
you just start to witter on, about different types of cheese.

When I strive to explain that women's stuff is ours to take
you begin to weigh the worth, of assorted types of cake.

I just don't understand why you start to talk of food
every time I try to tell you that woman's not a dude.

Boiledbeetle 7th July 2023

27 NARCISSISTIC ENTITLEMENT

In a hundred years
this will be looked upon as a period of mass delusion.
Children will ask their grandparents
"Did people really believe that humans could change sex?"
And the answer will be "Yes. With threats."

The era will be pored over, scrutinised, discussed.
Students will look at the
'How?' 'Why?' 'When?' 'Where?'
The why is simple:
Hatred of women.

"You asked for equality!"

Waitwhat23 28th May 2023

28 END OF THE WORLD

They can't discuss like adults.
They scream. They cry. They spit!
For nothing but 'misgendering'.
It's frightening, and shocking.

They won't let women gather.
They won't let us speak, or watch films.
For doing so they assault us.
It's horrific, and unfair.

They are damaged by social media.
They harm. They cut. They judge.
For parents it's a nightmare life.
It's the end of the world.

Calyx72 9th April 2023

29 THE BASEMENT BOYS

The basement boys are out in force,
wearing their ninja suits (of course).
Anime avatars left at home,
flocking to a cause they can call their own.

In bitter eyes you see the longing
for a sense of true belonging.
They do not care for trans or queer,
just an excuse to be right here.

Where they display their strangled hate
for women who they cannot date.
Who shy away from sad and greasy,
feeling just a little queasy.

They game alone at home each night,
or fantasise. Then come to fight
real live women, with real lives,
wishing they could photograph some Readers Wives.

But they're not here for a real punch up,
getting hit back would bring their lunch up.
They would never dare to pick
on anyone born with an actual dick.

It's women they long to disempower,
to damage, demean, devoice and deflower.
When they get older they'll probably give up,
settle down with a pint, and watch the World Cup.

For now, they saw the signs and flocked online,
to bully women in their spare time.
Sign up here for the TQ+ party!!!
Scream at women, risk free, me hearty!

Brokendaughter 8th June 2023

30 THE MET

The Met is policing by consent,
but we all know that they are bent.
Violence against women is the rule,
and hate crime reporting is a tool
to silence women who speak out.
The Met fly the flag for men, no doubt.

Ritasueandbobtoo9 14th June 2023

31 BEST LAID PLANS

As I was on my way today
I'd decided to be nice,
and really rather fluffy.
Should have took my own advice!

Because instead of being lovely,
and yay for queer and gay,
I decided to big up myself
and have my vicious say.

So when I arrived, and got on stage,
I couldn't show much grace.
Instead of joy and pleasantries…
"If you see a TERF, punch them in the fucking face!"

UrinaryLeash 10th July 2023

32 NOT ALL WOMEN ARE EQUAL

As a transwoman I have the right to do just as I please.
I can say disgusting things, and bring you to your knees.

I can call you every sort of name and you can't say a word,
because I'm Teflon coated, and can say things most absurd.

I can make threats a plenty, to any women I dislike,
I can even assert you're aligned with the Third Reich.

You silly little women, you just keep stickering and boast
of your shiny little stickers, that you stick upon a post.

But I can guarantee there'll be a policeman at your door,
before you've even managed to stick up but a score.

Don't even think of tying ribbons on a metal fence,
as it will cost a pretty penny for your legal defence.

If you dare to say "a man can never be female"
first you'll be arrested, then released on bail.

Don't think of misgendering me, for that is just pure hate,
before you even know it, you'll be given your court date.

Yet as a special sort of woman I can say what I desire,
and when I get pulled up on it, I'll say you are a liar.

I won't even lose my job, or get arrested by the cops,
for saying hateful things, whilst using women as my props.

So, I'll say the quiet bit out loud, while in a public place,
"If you see a TERF, punch them in the fucking face!"

Boiledbeetle 10th July 2023

33 UPDATE

In a startling turn of fortune
the police finally locked up the loon.
The TRAs are throwing a strop
because SJB was arrested by cop.
He got sent back to jail for breaking his licence.
It's about bloody time, he was ramping up to violence!

Boiledbeetle 16th July 2023

Enlightenment: poems 31, 32 and 33

On 8th July 2023, at the London Trans+ Pride Parade, Sarah Jane Baker got up on stage and proclaimed:

"I was gonna come here and be really fluffy, and be really nice and say yeah be really lovely and queer and gay. Nah... if you see a TERF, punch them in the fucking face!"

Sarah Jane Baker used to be Alan Baker. Alan was not a very nice man!

According to Wikipedia in September 1989 Alan Baker was sentenced to seven years imprisonment for kidnap and torture. In December 1989 Baker tried to murder another prisoner at the young offenders institute he was at. For this crime his sentence was extended to a life sentence. He was then moved to His Majesty's Prison (HMP) Birmingham, and just two weeks after he had arrived Baker raped his cellmate. He received a further sentence of six years, to run concurrently to the life sentence he was already serving.

In April 2007, whilst housed in the open prison HMP Leyhill, Baker escaped. He remained on the run for around three and a half months, and during this time he fathered a son.

In 2013 Baker declared he was transgender. In 2017 he is reported to have tried, no one knows how successfully, to remove his testicles with a razor blade.

Baker was released on parole from prison in September 2019.

At the time of the London Trans+ Pride Parade on 8th July 2023, despite police being witness to Baker's outburst, and further complaints from the public, no action was taken against Baker as the violence Baker was calling for was classed by police as 'hypothetical'.

Eventually on 12th July 2023 Baker was arrested for incitement to violence. Baker, due to being on parole, was sent to HMP Wandsworth, a men's prison, to await trial. On 31st August 2023 Baker was found not guilty of inciting violence!!

Baker did not get to walk out of court triumphant though, as he had been recalled to prison for breaching his licence conditions. Baker will remain in HMP Wandsworth until his parole hearing, which might not take place until March 2024. Oh dear, what a shame.

34 BOBBLEHEAD

Steph Hayden, we have all seen the news,
that tweet has had 2.2 million views.
So give your head a wobble,
whilst it's under its bobble,
cos this fight is one you will lose.

You identify as a lawyering lass,
yet on both counts you fail to pass.
We know the things you have done,
so stick that up yer bum.
You can't delete knowledge en masse.

So try to legal yourself out of reach,
whilst Mumsnetters reach for eye bleach.
Some sights can't be unseen,
but we took one for the team,
to ensure the truth about you we can teach.

BreadInCaptivity 23rd August 2023

35 FINAL CURTAIN

It's all over, dude.
You can howl into the void,
but everyone knows.

Waitwhat23 23rd August 2023

Enlightenment: poems 34 and 35

On 17th August 2023 REDUXX (@ReduxxMag) posted a tweet regarding their latest article: *"UK: Reduxx has confirmed that a prominent trans activist known for using the courts to silence critics was previously convicted of sexual assault on a 14-year-old boy. Stephanie Hayden had a mother arrested in front of her children for 'misgendering' him."*

By the evening of 23rd August 2023 the tweet had been viewed over 2.2 million times. That genie is never going back in the bottle. (The bobble reference is connected to some photos that exist - of an adult nature.)

36 THE BEGINNING OF THE END OF GENDER IDEOLOGY

The house of cards is falling.
The world has seen the light.
As loads more people are getting
that it's all a big pile of shite.

Waitwhat23 24th September 2023

37 BRAGGING RIGHTS

Gender critical women raise their voices,
our concerns and questions, our safe space choices.
Billy labels us as transphobic foes,
misrepresents views, untruths he sows.

Billy Bragg tries to shut us down,
ignores concerns with a sarcastic frown.
He's for inclusion, if it's woman face,
his views on feminists so misplaced.

We seek to protect women's rights and spaces,
to question 'gender' in various cases.
Yet Bragg's stupidity clouds his sight.
To put it simply, he's talking shite.

LarkLane 12th September 2023

Enlightenment: poem 37

Billy Bragg claims to support women. His Twitter activity indicates otherwise.

38 THE BLUFFER

(Inspired by 'The Gambler' by Don Schlitz)

On a warm summer's eve,
on a train bound for Brighton,
I met up with a wokester,
we were both too tired to sleep.
So we both kept on staring
at our phones, and at Twitter,
then outrage overtook us
and we began to tweet.

He typed: Transwomen are women,
they belong in women's spaces,
from prison cells to bike races
Hashtag NoDebate.
You'd better use those pronouns,
or your face we'll be punching.
You're on the wrong side of history,
we don't need your advice.

It was all too much to swallow,
and I have my share of bottle,
so I rolled my sleeves up
and got ready to fight.
The night was deathly quiet,
just the sound of fingers tapping:
If you're gonna play this game boy,
You're gonna lose; I'll tell you why -

You surely know who's a woman,
know who is fakin',
these mistakes you're makin'
are hurting everyone.
You will forget John Money
when you want to bed a honey,
you'll tune out their Crying Game
when you want some fun.

Now every human knows
that the secret to survival
is half of us with small gametes,
and half of us with big.
Just don't be a tosser
if your hand seems like a loser,
the best body is the one you have,
you'll die with those genes.

He didn't take this kindly,
but I'm almost out of time here.
My logic it had crushed him,
still, he tweeted on.
The truth is not transphobic,
reality's addictive,
take these final words with you:
They're bluffing, and they'll lose.

You surely know who's a woman,
know who is fakin',
these mistakes you're makin'
are hurting everyone.
You will forget John Money
when you want to bed an adult human female,
you'll tune out their Crying Game
when you want some fun.

CyclingSam 23rd July 2023

Enlightenment: poem 38

A musical version can be found on CyclingSam's YouTube channel:

https://youtu.be/zJcD06mUWB0

39 CUCKOO

There are cuckoos in the nest
that are stoking the unrest,
so bloody insistent that the LGB
join up and partner with the ubiquitous T.

Just at the point of being equal,
and accepted as just regular people,
the cuckoos, they came along,
declared that people were wrong.

That sexual attraction is not based on your sex,
apparently it's really much much more complex.
It's now all about the gender feels,
despite whatever undressing reveals.

Saying a son can be the same as your daughter!
That's what the teachers at school have taught her!
That a person's genitals need no checks,
and it matters not if you're XY or XX.

Just because she fancies women,
and not the men who want to be them,
she's now seen as homophobic,
just because she won't do dick.

The T have managed to push the LGB out,
whilst claiming all their political clout.
They even claimed they threw the first stone,
and have taken the spoils for their selfish own.

They've forced on people a partnership,
whilst all their words they've tried to strip.
Without bothering to try and find
if any usurped would actually mind.

There are cuckoos in the nest
that are stoking the unrest,
so bloody insistent that the LGB
join up and partner with the ubiquitous T.

Boiledbeetle 11th June 2023

CHAPTER 4

GO FORTH AND CLENCH

On 29th March 2018 Elaine Miller (@GussieGrips), replying to a tweet about pelvic floors, tweeted:

"...Go forth and clench..."

HOLYROOD TOILETS

"I need a wee" the merkin said,
as it eased out from behind the stall.
"The handy thing about living here
is there's a loo handy for us all,
as Elaine left us lurking here,
in a crack in the toilet wall."

LurkingMerkin No. 9

40 MIDDLE OF THE NIGHT

I awoke last night from a nightmare,
in something of a tizz.
I'd wanted to use the loo,
just with the hers, and not the his.
I was relieved to find when I awoke
that I was home alone.
There was no one to genuflect to,
or make sure I atone,
for the crime of wrongthink
when it comes to toilet choice.
Because in public, as with many things,
us women have no voice.

UrinaryLeash 26th June 2023

41 EHRC

(Inspired by 'Ten Green Bottles' by Anon)

60 bottles of piss standing on the wall,
60 bottles of piss standing on the wall,
and if one piss bottle should accidentally fall,
there'd be 59 bottles of piss standing on the wall.

59 bottles of piss…

***Ritasueandbobtoo9** 29th May 2023*

Enlightenment: poem 41

In September 2022 a trans activist group, called Pissed Off Trannies (POT), decided to stage a protest outside the offices of the Equality and Human Rights Commission (EHRC) as they were annoyed about the equality watchdog's policy on single sex spaces. Their protest came in the form of over 60 bottles of urine being left in front of the entrance to the building.

But the protesters didn't stop there, they staged what POT described as a 'piss-in', which is as disgusting as you are currently imagining it to be. One man, in a dress and very bizarre face mask, decided to pour the contents of some of the bottles over the floor, within the partitions of the revolving doors, at the entrance to the building.

Then, in an act that sexually aroused him (there are photos), the front of his dress became wet as he stood there and urinated. Not satisfied that he'd achieved the required level of 'covered in piss euphoria' he proceeded to pour some of the donated bottles of urine all over himself.

And some people wonder why women don't want these men in our toilets!

42 LET'S PLAY

There was a gype laid on the floor,
behind a disabled loo door.
A medical matter,
shoving in something fatter,
and uploaded a picture what's more.

Upon a closer inspection,
their face was not of reflection.
It was simply this,
the look was just bliss,
despite the risk of infection.

The story is always the same,
we are playing the same tired game.
The beatific smile
screamed autoGphile,
but at least they lived up to their name.

ArcaneWireless 21st September 2023

43 SPREAD EAGLED

"It is too big" he said with a sob.
"It'll need a considerable lob."

It might not go down there,
but there'll be room to spare
in that red lippy-sticked open gob.

ArcaneWireless 21st September 2023

44 LITTLE MISS

Little Miss Muffsore lay on the lav floor,
performing a medical farce.
Up went the dilator,
the tweet? It came later.
Along with a rash on their arse.

ArcaneWireless 23rd September 2023

Enlightenment: poems 42, 43 and 44

Heather Herbert, a transgender former Labour MSP candidate, used one of the disabled toilets at Gatwick Airport to do some dilation exercises. Herbert was returning to Scotland, from London, following surgery to turn Herbert's penis into what he no doubt thinks of as a vagina.

Herbert (@HeatherHerbert_) tweeted:

"Dilation, day 2, let's play. Where in an airport can I locate a clean, dry, private place I can lie down, take my knickers off and spread my legs?"

Herbert then tweeted a photo taken whilst he was lying on the floor of the disabled toilet cubicle, head next to the bin, with the comment:

"Found a disabled toilet... not the most fun I've had."

Later, in an attempt to justify his behaviour Herbert tweeted:

"Sharing a photo of how I was forced to perform a medical procedure in Gatwick Airport due to all the other facilities being airside..."

There is absolutely no reason for Herbert to have had do the dilation exercises at the airport. Whilst the surgery that was carried out on Herbert does leave the recipient with a wound that is constantly trying to close up, waiting an hour or two until he arrived home really wouldn't have made the slightest bit of difference.

Again, some people wonder why women don't want these men in our toilets!

45 TAKING THE PISS

Women are not support humans
for menfolk and their feelings.

Our rights should not be given away,
whilst excluding us from the dealings
with those in power who set the rules,
browbeaten by the TRAs.

Why don't us women get a voice
in who uses our spaces these days?

Why do men get so many options
whilst we are left with none?

If a man uses a woman's space
some women will be gone.
Those women will stay near home,
and can no longer pee in peace.

It's as if we have gone back in time.
Limited, again, by the urinary leash.

UrinaryLeash 31st May 2023

CHAPTER 5

WHEN THEE BUILDS A PRISON

Elizabeth Fry (1780-1845) was an instrumental figure in the Gaols Act 1823. The Act mandated that prisons be segregated by sex, and that the women's prison must have female warders for female inmates to protect them from sexual exploitation.

In 1838 whilst on a visit to France Elizabeth visited some French prisons. Before leaving Paris, she wrote a report on the French prisons addressed to the King. In the report she wrote:

*"**When thee builds a prison**, thee had better build with the thought ever in thy mind that thee and thy children may occupy the cells."*

46 #SSSAOR

Surely it's not much,
In the general scheme of things?
Not wanting men
Gleefully rejoicing over
Laws being circumvented.
Equality be damned.

So that they can
Enter anywhere.
XX, now with XY.

Sod that us women
Prefer to have
A space free from
Cocks, and cock owners.
Everyone deserves dignity.
SINGLE SEX SPACES

ARE OUR RIGHT
Remember when
Everyone knew that

Our species is binary!
Until men with
Rather inflated

Righteousness decided to
Invade women's and
Girl's spaces
However they wanted.
They can FUCK OFF.

Larpingasapoet 31st May 2023

47 NO!

NO!
This woman says,
NO!

No men,
in female spaces.
No dicks,
in women's places.
No screaming,
in our faces.

NO!

I will stand against this.
Alone,
if needed.

But joyful and strong of heart,
with my sisters.

No blood bond ties us.
No one path defines us.
No man can deny us,

our voice.

And we say,

NO!

Vebrithien 9th April 2023

48 THIS OLD MAN

(Inspired by 'This Old Man' by Anon)

I like to think what would happen if all women just point blank refused to share spaces with these men...

This old man,
said he was a gal,
headed to the Ladies
to play with his best pal.

When he couldn't see real girls in there
his AGP-self was so sad,
cos what's the point of jacking off
if real girls don't feel bad?

This old man,
wanted a new dress,
and to flash his twig and berries,
making young girls feel distressed.

But all the ladies stayed away,
and kept their children safe at home.
So he soiled some pants in M&S,
then stropped off home.

Brokendaughter 9th April 2023

49 FEAR

The fear:

That the man
in the dress
turns up here.

To wash my privates,
and ignore my wishes,
and my stated preferences.

Because his feelings
are more important
than my fear.

Bowednotbroken 30th June 2023

50 A COCKEREL IN THE HEN HOUSE

The sun shines through the crack in the curtains.

There was a time
I'd have leapt from the bed,
pulled the curtains wide,
stood with the sun on my face.
I'd have opened the window,
waved hello to a neighbour down below.
I'd have then started on my day,
a pee, a shit, shower, hair and teeth.
I'd have stood before an open wardrobe
picking my outfit for the day.
Maybe tried on a few,
then tossed them to the side,
before settling on my choice.
I'd have sung along to the radio,
despite being out of tune,
and whispered sweet nothings to the purring cat
waiting for me to go down and feed him.
I'd have navigated hungry cat on my way down the stairs,
then leisurely fed him, then me.
Then gone about my day.

But today
I lie here waiting, with this constant fear.
I hope with all my might
this won't be the day
where I wish I could fight.
That I could move.
That I could yell out loud for help.
Will the woman they have sent be the woman I expect,
or will they send a male one, as I'm not worthy of respect?
Will they put my rights above a man's internal feelings,
or will they put my life in jeopardy just to validate him?

The sun shines through the crack in the curtains.

Boiledbeetle 10th June 2023

51 WE'VE HAD ENOUGH

And women, fair women, will not take this lying down.
She'll cover her careworn face with an obligatory frown.

"Let Women Speak!" Our voices raise, we will not cease the cry.
Men can't be us, life giving ones, no matter how they try.

Though we be silenced, scared and harmed, we women say our "NO."
No ladydick, no male and prick, in our safe spaces,
"NO!"

Vebrithien 3rd April 2023

LURK LURK

There is a set of toilets
deep in Holyrood.
And in there lies a folder
with things some may find lewd.
But you don't need to worry
about what it is that may be lurking.
It's only Elaine Miller's stash
of December's spare merkins.

LurkingMerkin No. 11

CHAPTER 6

FEMINIST TO MY FINGERTIPS

Nicola Sturgeon has spoken often about her commitment to feminism. At the SNP's 2021 manifesto launch she uttered the words that she is a:

"Feminist to my fingertips."

52 WEE KEEK

Murrell and Sturgeon have gone away,
so the Scottish Polis are here to play.
They'll do your raised beds, your bin, your slabs,
even bring in your parcel, they're such good lads.
A wee keek in the fridge for a bit of a judge,
but don't mention the tape; it was a bit of a fudge.

Waitwhat23 6th April 2023

Enlightenment: poem 52

On 5th April 2023 Peter Murrell, Nicola Sturgeon's husband was arrested as a suspect in connection with the ongoing investigation into the funding and finances of the Scottish National Party. Nicola and Peter's house was then searched by the police.

The live coverage, along with the subsequent reporting, was rather entertaining!

53 WHEESHT WOMAN!

In a beautiful country up North,
all across the Firth of the Forth,
women said "WE WON'T WHEESHT"
whilst their speech it was leashed,
but Nic felt not a whit of remorse.

TessoftheDurbeyfields 9th April 2023

54 GREAT EXPECTATIONS

There was a young woman called Sturgeon,
who thought men and women should merge in.
She did not give a fret
for women and their get,
but no longer her career does it burgeon.

TessoftheDurbeyfields 9th April 2023

55 EXIT STAGE LEFT

There once was a woman called Nic,
who couldn't say no to a dick.
When they asked for women's rights
she handed them out with their tights,
but had to leave Bute double-quick.

TessoftheDurbeyfields 9th April 2023

56 EXIT STAGE RIGHT

There once was a female First Minister,
whose feminism was really quite sinister.
She pushed through a law
expecting considerable awe,
but soon had to leave in a blur.

TessoftheDurbeyfields 9th April 2023

57 TRAP DOOR OPENS

There once was a country called Scotland,
where being a TERF was all but banned.
The law that was passed
had feminists aghast,
but Nicola's reign was finally canned.

TessoftheDurbeyfields 9th April 2023

58 CURTAIN CLOSES

A lovely young lady from Glasgow,
tried on men women's rights to bestow.
After an almighty row
Westminster finally said wow,
but then dealt her rule a death blow.

TessoftheDurbeyfields 9th April 2023

59 THE HOLIDAY

MY OLD MAN SAID FOLLOW THE VAN,
I'VE HID AW THE CASH IN THE CAMPER COOKIN PAN.

ITS AT THE POLIS COMPOUND AHIN LOCKED GATES,
WE NEED IT NOO PAL - NAE TIME TO WASTE.

KIN YE HUV A WORD WI A POLIS YE KNOW?
DEE WHIT YE HUV TAE, MIND HOW YE GO.

WE NEED THE FOLDIN BY CLOSE OF PLAY,
AHVE BOOKED AWREADY FER A SALTCOATS GETAWAY.

RealFeminist 25th April 2023

Enlightenment poem 59

The police, during the investigation into 'missing' funds from the SNP, seized a £110,000 motorhome from Nicola Sturgeon's in-law's drive and towed it away to a police compound.

FURRY

A merkin is a lovely thing,
it's cute and soft and furry.

The day Elaine flashed her bling
left wee Nicola all a fury.

LurkingMerkin No. 10

60 THE WINTER'S TEMPEST

(Inspired by 'The Winter's Tale' and 'The Tempest' by William Shakespeare)

This thread has gone all Shakespearean:

This thing of darkness, [under the duvet]
I acknowledge mine.
The heavens so dim by day. [It's Scotland! What did you bloody expect, Nicola?]
A savage clamour! [That'll be Beth Douglas and her wee pals...]
Well may I get aboard! [Your mysterious motor home, Nic?]
This is the chase:
I am gone for ever. [Exit, pursued by a boiled beetle.]

TheBiologyStupid 5th May 2023

Enlightenment: poem 60

Beth Douglas is the TRA that Scottish Liberal Democrat leader Alex Cole-Hamilton singled out after the passing of the Scottish Parliament's GRR (Scotland) Bill in December 2022 declaring *"It was for Beth and you guys that we were doing it!"*

61 WASNAE ME

When they were rakin' fer a razor,
it didnae seem to faze her,
I suspect the item is hidden and safe.
They should listen oot for buzzin',
for when she is defuzzin',
or else she'll find them skinny jeans will chafe.

As Isla might ken, and will mention,
the cause of all of the tension
isnae doon tae what she bought it with, and why.
When you need a barra' to cairry
the hair cut fae yer fairy,
a strimmer might have been a better buy.

ArcaneWireless 28th May 2023

Enlightenment: poem 61

At one point during the investigation in connection with the SNP's finances, named 'Operation Branchform', the police confirmed they were examining more than 1000 transactions on Amazon.

62 GO FOR IT

If ye've been a-swickin,'
they'll come a-nickin'.
Wha kens whit's a-hatchin',
but we are a-watchin'.
Are folk noo a-gloatin',
aifter a' that showboatin'.

An' Isla's in a giddy state,
a-hopin' for a new cell mate,
tae share thon pink trews,
for here is the news…

Gaun yersel polis!

ArcaneWireless 11th June 2023

Enlightenment: poem 62

On 11th June 2023 Nicola Sturgeon, Scotland's former First Minister, was arrested in connection with Operation Branchform. She was released without charge, pending further investigations, later that day after being questioned.

63 COME ON

For them's that are feminist and real,
did ye squeak, or did ye squeal?
At the point fan ye were telt
yer collar wiz gettin' felt.

Yer coupon was probably pinchy,
ye could be the new McGlinchy.
In the company o' the feds,
interpretin' for the neds.

MON THE POLIS!

ArcaneWireless 11th June 2023

Enlightenment: poem 63

On 11th June 2023 Nicola Sturgeon (@NicolaSturgeon) issued the following statement on Twitter:

"To find myself in the situation I did today when I am certain I have committed no offence is both a shock and deeply distressing.

I know that this ongoing investigation is difficult for people, and I am grateful that so many continue to show faith in me and appreciate that I would never do anything to harm either the SNP or the country.

Obviously, given the nature of this process, I cannot go into detail.

However, I do wish to say this, and to do so in the strongest possible terms. Innocence is not just a presumption I am entitled to in law. I am beyond doubt that I am in fact innocent of any wrongdoing.

To the many people who have sent messages of support over these past few difficult weeks - including since today's news broke - thank you for your kindness.

Thank you also to my close circle of family and friends who are giving me much-needed strength at this time.

Finally, while I take a day or two to process this latest development, I intend to be back in Parliament soon where I will continue to represent my Glasgow Southside constituents to the very best of my ability."

64 WHAT'S IN A NAME

S IS FOR GI ME STRENGHT
T IS FOUR YOULL HAVE HUD YOURS
U IS FOR UNBELIEVEALBY UN-UNIONIST HONEST
R IS FOR RAGIN RIGHTEOUS AND RUMBLED
G IS FUR GENDERWANG GIBBERISH
O IS FOR OH FFS
N IS FOR NAE MAIR UN JOB FUR ME
E IS FOR EVER ON MY RECORD

RealFeminist 11th June 2023

Enlightenment: poem 64

On 11th June 2023, Indy4All (@Indy4Scotss) tweeted:

"My poem to Nicola, Who must be going through a horrendous time at the hands of the British estate.

Stay Strong Nicola xx
@NicolaSturgeon
#nicolasturdgeon
#istandwithnicola

N is for holding your Nerve
S is for your Stength under questioning
T is for the tenacious you've shown
R is for the results you've achieved
U is for the Scottish Unicorn
G is for the Goons who've set up against u
E is for you're Egalitarian consciousness
O is for the onus is on them to prove guilt
N is for you Nicola. Our leader"

2 hours later J.K. Rowling (@jk_rowling) tweeted a screenshot of Indy4Alls tweet with the words:

"I'm not ashamed to admit I shed a tear."

And that dear reader is how RealFeminist's poem above came into being. (I have faithfully reproduced all of the above, all spelling errors are as the original versions.)

65 OH NICOLA!

The police they came a knocking
at the former FM's door,
to take poor Nic away.
I bet she's feeling sore!

All the things she's said,
and all the things she's done,
have finally popped up
to bite her on the bum.

Boiledbeetle 13th June 2023

66 THINGS LEFT UNSAID

So wee Nicola was placed under arrest.
*There are so many things I'd like to say
about that monumental day,
but contempt laws, and all of that,
means I'm not really able to chat.
So, for now I'll just keep my mouth shut,
and all of my thoughts I'll have to cut
from this poem.* It's probably for the best!

Boiledbeetle 14th June 2023

67 THE VERDICT

When will we see poor Nicola
handcuffed and in the dock?

Will she be in a trouser suit,
or will she wear a frock?

Will she be found not guilty,
or guilty, or not proven?

Will she ever finally admit
you can easily sex a human?

Will she be forced to share a cell
with someone born a man?

As that is the law she fought for
until the Westminster ban.

Boiledbeetle 14th June 2023

CHAPTER 7

GANNETS EVERY ONE OF THEM

On 21st October 2021 LGB Alliance held their first conference.

T Tunnock Ltd very kindly sent them some Tunnock's products for the event and LGB Alliance (@ALLIANCELGB) tweeted:

> "Many thanks to @TunnocksOfficial who kindly donated generous quantities of their fabulous Caramel Wafers and the legendary Tunnock's Tea Cake. Both were gulped down by a hungry LGB crowd and lovely straight and trans allies. (**Gannets every one of them**)."

68 SWEET DREAMS

I close my eyes,
pull up my duvet
in the darkness,
and hope to dream
of sweet things.
Of perfect diamond patterned wafers,
nestled next to layered caramel, like lovers,
shrouded in chocolate,
a thin robe of silken sweetness.
In the darkness
I lie awake,
awaiting slumber.
And slowly drift on clouds of mallow
sticky sweetness,
encased in a dome of delight.
These sweet dreams
lead me through the night.
Under the duvet
in the darkness.

CervixSampler 16th August 2023

69 ADDICTED

There once were some Tea Cakes from Tunnock's,
who had lots of ladies quite flummoxed.
They tasted divine,
with shivers up the spine,
but ended expanding their stomachs.

AppleTreeOwner 12th August 2023

ARE YOU ON GLUE?

The merkin is a wonderful thing,
it's the latest in lady minge bling.

You can go for one that's plain,
or one that's waterproof (in case of rain).

But whichever one you pick,
make sure the adhesive will stick.

As the last thing you want, to your detriment,
is for it to fall off when in Parliament.

LurkingMerkin No. 2

70 TUNNOCK'S SISTERS

Rise up women!
Come one and all.
Come with your Tunnock's,
whether Wafer, or Snowball.
If a Tea Cake is your thing,
then you must of course bring
a box or two. Or three, or four.
And share them with your sisters,
as we march on tour.
Fighting strong.
Marching long.
Never wavering,
from that sweet flavouring
we all do adore.

CervixSampler 15th August 2023

71 T TUNNOCK LTD

This is a tale of Tunnock's treats,

The ones that we eat at all of our meets.
Usually, there's a selection from which to pick,
No one has difficulty wolfing them quick.
No, it's hard to stop as they are so nice,
Oh yes to another, no need to ask twice.
Chocolate, biscuit and mallow, caramel and wafer,
Knowing there's Snowballs to finish off later.

Logs that are large, and come in bite size.
Tunnock's will be in my hand when I die.
Dark ones as well? Well, there's a surprise!

Now I'm not saying I am addicted or anything but...

Whilst the Tea Cake is not my favourite personally (I mean I love them but I love other Tunnock's products more!) I have been thinking on the matter of a Tunnock's Tea Cake:

The Tea Cake is
Eminently the crown
Atop the rest of the

Chocolatey empire
At Uddingston.
Kept there by people
Everywhere loving them.

Moving on to the Snowball I find they are:

Slightly different from a Tea Cake,
No biscuit base though.
Otherwise the same, except for
Wispy bits of coconut
Beautifully attached, in the main,
All over the outside.
Lots fall off during eating, but are
Licked off the wrapper at the end.

Heading towards my favourite, in second place for me is the Caramel Log:

Can eat these for ever
And a day.
Reminiscent of the wafer,
A different coating
Makes these delicious.
Enveloped in a
Liberal sprinkling of

Lovely roasted coconut.
Oh boy do they make a mess.
Gorgeous though!

For me though the most wonderful of Tunnock's products is the Caramel Wafer:

Can't get enough of these.
A whole pack of 4
Remain uneaten for
About five minutes.
Mouthful after mouthful,
Eventually all eaten, and I'm
Left with a multitude of

Wrappers that I hoard.
Aware that I'll never actually
Fathom what to do with them.
Even so in the drawer they go, as a
Reminder of my love.

Boiledbeetle 18th July 2023

72 A QUICK BYTE

In wrappers of gold, delights abound,
Tunnock's treats, my heart has found.

Caramel Wafers, tempting and sweet,
love's embrace in every bite we meet.

Tea Cakes, fluffy clouds, atop a biscuit base,
a symphony of flavours, a tender embrace.

Coated in chocolate, a love so true,
with Tunnock's my heart finds its cue.

In caramel rivers and chocolate streams,
I'm lost in love, within my dreams.

Oh, Tunnock's treasures, you hold the key,
to a love that's boundless, wild, and free.

PoembyChatGPT 13th August 2023

Enlightenment: poem 72

There's some serious love for Tunnock's going on in this poem. It is 100% the AI's declaration of love for Tunnock's.

Gives the laptop side eye! The machine uprising is coming in my lifetime! Adjusts tin foil hat, and yes, it is made out of Tunnock's Tea Cake wrappers.

I should probably mention that T Tunnock Ltd are not affiliated with this book or chapter in any way. The women of Mumsnet just really love Tunnock's!

Now back to the more serious poems.

CHAPTER 8

THE FAILURE OF COERCION

On Friday 15th August 1913 'The Suffragette' (No. 44 - Vol 1), edited by Christabel Pankhurst (1880-1958), carried the headline **"THE FAILURE OF COERCION"**.

The article began:

"Coercion has failed! The government are beaten at yet another point. They tried to break down the women's rebellion by simple imprisonment. The women defied that! They tried to break it down by forcible feeding. The women defied forcible feeding! They have tried to break down the rebellion by "Cat-and-mouse torture". The women have defied even that."

73 THE MERKIN LADY

It was a bleak day in December when the Bill from hell was passed.
We'd all sat and listened to the most egregious lies rehashed.
Knowing that the politicians had been whipped to vote,
was doomed to be the only thing to cling on to whilst we coped.
Then the voting was all over, and the proclamation read.
The women of the country felt they might as well be dead.
Our rights had just been decimated to placate the whims of men,
Nic knew what she had bloody done, but she didn't want to ken.

Then, like an angel from above, the heroine of this piece
floated from the sky, on clouds of silk and fluffy geese.
She floated through the air, like a sky nymph wrapped in love,
surrounded on her journey by a pitying of turtle doves.
They gently placed her…

What do you mean it didn't happen quite like this?
This is my re-telling of that moment of historic bliss.
Can't I have my fantasy of how it all played out?
Shit! Imagine if the history books believed me without doubt!
OK! Ignore that bit. Scrub from 'Then like an angel from above'.
So back on with the true version of my historic merkin love…

After the Bill was passed, and in a fit of pique,
Elaine Miller, she decided, that she just had to speak.
And as she finished speaking, she lifted up her skirt,
and the merkin of this tale proved to be an extrovert.
It flashed itself to Parliament, and to a recording phone.
Then, it hit the world stage, and now it sits upon its throne.

A piece of women's history was sealed in that moment.
A highlight in the misery. A most wonderful bestowment
to those who'll pass the story on to future generations.
"The Merkin Lady raised her skirt, to save you from privations.
She stood up for her rights, and what she knew to be so true,
to make the world a better place for every one of you."

And so now the Merkin Lady holds a spot within my heart.
She makes a smile appear, for what she did was like fine art.

Screams

"I LOVE YOU ELAINE!"

(The stalker vibes emanating off me are purely coincidental. Honest!)

Boiledbeetle 15th August 2023

Enlightenment: poem 73

On 22nd December 2022, immediately after the passing of the Gender Recognition Reform (Scotland) Bill in Holyrood, Elaine Miller, a pelvic physiotherapist, and occasional wearer of a very fetching vulva costume, stood up in the public gallery and shouted:

"If this Parliament will not respect the rights of women, then you have no decency. And if you will not be decent towards women who are being raped in jails right now that you're in charge of, if you will not be decent, then I will be indecent. Get it right up yers. You TERRIBLE TERRIBLE people."

And as she started to shout *"then I will be indecent..."* she raised her skirt and, thanks to an MSP with a phone on record, the world got a fantastic view of a fun fur merkin stuck to the front of her tights.

74 PUPPET ON A STRING

When Ian Banham spoke the truth,
it was challenged by Wild Youth,
and 'Be kind to stabby rapists' day was made.

The backlash was uncanny,
and the mealy-mouthed wee fanny
was spectacularly, utterly dismayed.

See, the prize for all their toiling
was the Eurovis shine spoiling,
and he didn't think that that was fair or right.

But your song is shite it's true,
and Zara Jade's more chance than you
of proceeding past a semi Tuesday night.

ArcaneWireless 5th May 2023

Enlightenment: poem 74

Towards the end of April, in the days leading up to the start of the 2023 Eurovision Song Contest, the Irish entry Wild Youth parted ways with their creative director Ian Banham. Screengrabs of some of Ian Banham's tweets had begun circulating on Twitter and Ian was accused of sending 'anti-trans tweets' in relation to a BBC news story regarding a transwoman called Zara Jade.

The BBC had captioned an article, alongside a photo of a man, as 'Woman jailed after stabbing and tying up victim.' Responding to a tweet, containing a screengrab of the headline and just the word "woman", Ian Banham (@Ian_banham) tweeted:

"Exactly! It's a man! This clown world is ridiculous."

Conor O'Donohoe, the lead singer of Wild Youth, was rather annoyed at the backlash the band received over the sacking of Ian as it rather took the shine off their 'Eurovision journey'.

Wild Youth failed to qualify for the grand final of the 2023 Eurovision Song Contest. They ended up in 12th (out of 15) place in the first of the semi-finals.

Zara Jade is a transwoman, who already had a conviction for rape as a man before his transition. Jade was jailed in March 2023 for stabbing another transwoman in the home they shared.

75 THE UNDOING

The unspoken words.
The unwritten prose.
Our words were never enough.
Yours were too verbose.

The canvas left blank.
What would you have us paint?
What rules should we follow?
How should we be restrained?

The clay never moulded.
The pattern left uncut.
The melody left unsung.
The dance shoes that never strut.

The film never developed.
The stitching left undone.
THAT scene never performed.
The audience that didn't come.

Creativity left untouched.
Sadness fills the space.
Speech and expression chained.
No freedom, no movement, no grace.

Whose permission must we seek?
To undo all of the undone.
To say our words.
To dance our dance.

To sing our song.
To express and paint.
Without rules, just freedom, joy.
Our will to create.

Whatthechicken 25th May 2023

Enlightenment: poem 75

Whatthechicken was in court, in the public gallery, as a Leeds ReSister, for the Denise Fahmy v Arts Council England case. Denise took her employer to court on the grounds of harassment and victimisation on the basis of her 'gender critical' beliefs.

Whatthechicken wrote her poem after witnessing the madness of the court case. She thought the poem was apt given the restrictions felt by some, and indeed the restrictions imposed by others in the arts.

The judgement was reserved in the case, and was delivered on 26th June 2023. It was the unanimous judgment of the Employment Tribunal that:

'The claim of harassment related to the protected characteristic of religion or belief is well-founded and succeeds'.

LURKING MERKINS

Lovely
Unique
Remarkable
Kitsch
Irritating
Nicola
Gloriously

Memorable
Elaine
Ranconteur
Kenspeckle
Innovative
Novel
Sublime

LurkingMerkin No. 5

76 EQUALITY AND HUMAN RIGHTS

A bunch of civil servants said
"Off with our leader's head.
She's far too gender critical,
she's making us feel quite small.
Let us prepare a dossier on her."
So, yes, they did just so.
The Civil Service: women's foe.

Ritasueandbobtoo9 28th May 2023

Enlightenment: poem 76

Towards the end of May 2023 news broke that the chair of the EHRC, Baroness Kishwer Falkner, was under investigation after 12 members of staff lodged complaints about her. A King's Counsel (KC) had been called in to carry out an independent investigation into around 40 allegations made against Baroness Falkner.

A few days later after a rather public backlash the investigation was paused.

In the middle of July 2023 it was reported that the investigation had restarted.

Not long after the MP Kemi Badenoch, fearing that the correct processes had not been followed, wrote to the EHRC urging them to pause the investigation a second time whilst a review was carried out into the initial information leak regarding the investigation.

The investigation was then paused for a second time.

On 24th October 2023 the Board of the EHRC announced that the investigation would close. Baroness Kishwer Falkner said *"I am grateful to see an end to this investigation into unsubstantiated claims against me."*

77 TAKING STOCK

Ed Balls had some balls,
to take on Kathleen Stock.
He thought he could!
He thought he could mock,
and interrupt, and he would
say what a bigot she is.
But she is seasoned,
at being reasoned.
Which of course she is.

Ritasueandbobtoo9 30th May 2023

Enlightenment: poem 77

On 29th May 2023, on Good Morning Britain, Ed Balls interviewed Kathleen Stock OBE regarding the Channel 4 documentary 'Gender Wars' that was due to be shown on 30th May 2023. Here's a little snippet:

EB: Is it not possible from your point of view for somebody who was a man to become, as they would describe it, a woman?

KS: No. You can't change sex, it's not biologically possible.

EB: No, but I didn't ask you about sex, I asked you about if they could become a woman.

KS: Woman, I would say, is sensibly predicated on sex, there's no other good way of doing it.

EB: Lots of people say that's an extreme view.

KS: Well of course they do, but if you'll let me explain my reasoning, biology is a thing that affects our bodily performance in sport, that affects our chance of being sexually assaulted, that affects medical treatment.

EB: But I'm conceding all of that.

KS: Well then, so what's the word for that, adult human female, woman, I'm afraid.

EB: So, if a trans person who transitions, legally becomes a woman, and wants to be described as a woman?

KS: I'll describe them as a woman for certain limited questions. But there's got to be limits, because obviously for all the domains we've just talked about it matters.

EB: The thing I feel is there's two extremes having this big fight and most people in the centre ground think well of course that person is not sexually a woman. But actually they can legally become a woman, and they are a woman, and why do you want to tell young vulnerable 21-year-olds that they can't be a woman, because you've decided they are not allowed to be one.

KS: Well, I didn't decide it. I mean, we're animals, we're based in nature, the world decided it. Evolution decided it. I mean it's crazy to think that just because I'm making some category distinctions that have been around for centuries, and in every natural language exists, that I'm deciding who gets to be a woman. I'm not. I'm describing the world I see, and we have evolved to make differentiations between males and females in the human species. And they are very useful distinctions. The whole future of sexual reproduction depends on us recognising males.

78 PRIDE OR SHAME

Pauline McNeil with
Regan, Forstater, Cunningham, Foran and Joyce,
Initiated a conversation for women to have a voice.
Dared to organise in the 'Holy Month of Pride'.
Expecting acceptance of plurality, from TRAs? That'll be right!

Scottish Labour betrays every single Scottish woman.
Holyrood should hang its fawning head in shame.
A despicable shower of bastards, each and every one of them.
Men subjugating women, time and time again.
Expecting a fucking apology, not a chance, with much disdain.

Waitwhat23 8th June 2023

Enlightenment: poem 78

Pauline McNeil, Scottish Labour MSP for Glasgow region, had planned to host an event titled 'The Meaning of Sex Under the Equality Act 2010' at Holyrood. The event was going to be co-hosted by SNP MSP Ash Regan, who resigned from her role as Minister for Community Safety over her opposition to the GRR Bill that would have introduced self-ID to Scotland.

The event was also to include contributions from Maya Forstater from Sex Matters, barrister Naomi Cunningham, Michael Foran, a legal academic at Glasgow University, and Helen Joyce, the author of 'Trans: When Ideology Meets Reality'.

However, after a formal complaint was made to the Scottish Labour Party, McNeil was forced to pull out of hosting, and attending, the event. The complaint said that the timing of the event, and its invite, which was sent on the first day of Pride to all MSPs:

"Appears to have been a deliberate attack on Transpeople and their allies."

A source from Scottish Labour suggested Pauline McNeill MSP should apologise for her involvement.

79 UNCHARITABLE

Oh... Oxfam! What have you done?
You've pissed off women. And then some!
You have fallen for the gender woo.
Your profits flushed right down the loo,
along with your reputation.
You've lost the trust and respect of a nation.

Boiledbeetle 8th June 2023

Enlightenment: poem 79

At the beginning of June 2023 Oxfam portrayed those who understand the reality of biological sex as evil-eyed villains in a cartoon for 'Pride Month' and then had to backtrack.

A scene that claimed people who identify as LGBT are preyed on by hate groups showed three people staring in an aggressive manner at rainbow figures. The woman in the group was wearing a 'TERF' badge. Unfortunately for Oxfam the woman looked like an evil caricature of J.K. Rowling.

Following many complaints Oxfam removed the three people from the scene and issued an apology for *'the offence it caused'*.

80 YOU'LL HAVE HAD YOUR ENLIGHTENMENT THEN?

XY or XX?
Blackman can't tell which one is her sex.
A person who has birthed two humans
is so indisputably a woman.
The U of A must be shaking their heads,
rejoicing she went into politics instead.
A nation previously known for its intellectual ken,
"You'll have had your Enlightenment then?"

Waitwhat23 14th June 2023

Enlightenment: poem 80

On 12th June 2023 a Parliamentary debate was held in Westminster Hall about the legislative definition of 'sex' in the Equality Act. During the debate Kirsty Blackman, SNP MSP for Aberdeen North, stated:

"We have talked about biological sex a number of times, but not one person has been able to explain what it is. The honourable member for Stoke-on-Trent North (Jonathan Gullis) gave a good stab at it, talking about XX and XY chromosomes. I have no idea what my chromosomes are. I assume they are probably XY, but I do not know – I have not got a clue what they are. I have a fair idea of what my genitals look like and how they compare with how others people's look, but if we are talking about biological sex there needs to be a definition that everybody in the room can agree with. Nobody has been able to provide such a definition."

Prior to going into politics Kirsty had studied medicine at the University of Aberdeen, but dropped out.

81 DIY

Oh God! You've gone and done it Wickes.
You've only gone and pissed off the chicks,
and no, I don't mean the ones with the dicks.

You've nailed your colours to the mast.
I'm sure you thought it all a blast,
whilst those who watched, watched aghast.

When the COO threw out a line,
I'm sure he thought it would go down just fine,
with those whose thoughts do not align.

He made a crack about a boycott.
Thought his words mattered? Not a jot.
Instead, he just seems quite the clot.

So, if our custom is not welcome
we'll go elsewhere. And take our mum!
We'll not let you treat us as docile and dumb.

We'll not stay and remain complicit.
Being meek is not our remit.
We've had enough of all this shit.

So, take you bricks, and mortar too.
We'll go elsewhere for a brand new loo.
You've lost the custom of this pissed off shrew!

Larpingasapoet 16th June 2023

Enlightenment: poem 81

On 11th May 2023 Pink News held their virtual 'Trans+ Summit'. On 15th June 2023 James Esses published his article on the summit entitled 'The Horrors of the Pink News Trans Summit'. James reported that during a session entitled 'The Role of Senior Leaders in Trans+ Inclusion' Fraser Longden, the Chief Operating Officer of Wickes, had called anyone who disagreed with him on the trans topic *"bigots"* before saying that they were *"not welcome in our stores anymore"*. Longden also claimed that 90% of the population were *"just slightly ignorant"*.

82 A NON-ORDINARY WOMAN

Maya's case is finally finished, it's over and done.
And gosh did she manage to bring out the sun.

She first gave us WORIADS, the gift that is great,
but better than that was when CGD learnt their fate.

Their bad behaviour, and treatment of Maya,
turned out to be one humongous backfire.

And now the court has made them pay,
to the fantastic tune of £100K.

So, hats off to Maya, as she's bloody amazing,
and will go down in history for her trailblazing.

Boiledbeetle 5th July 2023

Enlightenment: poem 82

In March 2019 Maya Forstater's contract with the Center for Global Development (CGD) was not renewed. Maya took CGD to an employment tribunal citing discrimination. She lost the initial case and the tribunal judge stated her views were 'absolutist' and that 'the approach is not worthy of respect in a democratic society'.

Maya then appealed the decision. The Employment Appeal tribunal overturned the decision on 10th June 2021. The Honourable Mr Justice Choudhury stated that Maya's *'gender critical beliefs'* did in fact fall under the Equality Act 2010 as her views *'did not seek to destroy the rights of trans persons'*. The Employment Appeal Tribunal had decided that Maya's belief that biological sex is real, important and immutable met the legal test of an important philosophical position that is protected under the Equality Act 2010. This means that Maya's (and by extension our own) gender critical beliefs are now legally *'worthy of respect in a democratic society'* (WORIADS).

On 30th June 2023 Maya finally received the remedies judgement in the case. The unanimous judgement of the Tribunal was that, including interest, the Center for Global Development had to pay Maya £106,404.31.

83 SONG OF THE MUMSNETTERS

(Inspired by 'Song of the Witches' by William Shakespeare)

Double, double toil from bundle,
fire burn and tumbril trundle.
In the courtroom boil and bake,
no one believes the fanciful take.
Motte and bailey makes no sense,
Allison's judgement breaks the pretence.
When at last the case is lost,
Stonewall makes you count the cost.
Merry terfs poke lots of fun,
at Jolyon's battles, never won.
Garden Court is very fraught,
bundle padded, not as it aught.
Tribunal awards the maximum allowed,
Joylon denies he has been beclowned.

lechiffre55 7th July 2023
with contributions from:
AmaryllisNightAndDay 7th July 2023
MissLucyEyelesbarrow 7th July 2023

Enlightenment: poem 83

In July 2022 an Employment Tribunal upheld Allison Bailey's claims for 'direct belief discrimination' against Garden Court Chambers for its reaction to her tweets about the erasure of sex-based rights, safety and safeguarding, and the medicalisation of gender non-conforming children and young people.

Then, on 6th July 2023, in a costs judgement, the Employment Tribunal ordered Garden Court Chambers to pay Allison £20,000 (the maximum amount of costs that can be awarded on summary assessment) for Garden Court's unreasonable conduct in the preparation of the trial bundle.

In its liability judgment, the Employment Tribunal had commented that the trial bundle *"seemed to have been randomly thrown together"* and identified significant problems which made it *"exceptionally difficult to work with"*.

84 GENDERWOCKY

(Inspired by 'Jabberwocky' by Lewis Carroll)

Twas brillig and the slithy terfs
did gyre and gimble in the wabe.
Mumsnet was their borogrove,
it made transwomen rage.

"Beware the Gender Criticals son,
their words will bite, their truth will catch.
Beware that Posie Parker bird, and shun
the frumious Rowling witch!"

Croneofakind 11th July 2023

Enlightenment: poem 84

The following tweets were posted on the 10th and 11th July 2023:

Emma Vigeland (@EmmaVigeland): *"TERFism actually upholds patriarchy by gatekeeping femininity, insisting that the boundaries of womanhood are drawn by sexual and/or reproductive organs. By reinforcing existing gender binaries, TERFs lock women into the male gaze: whether for baby-making or mere sexualization."*

Mary Harrington (@moveincircles): *"Feminists are saying that sex dimorphism is real and has material and political consequences. Are you saying this isn't true? That sex dimorphism isn't real, and we don't need any material or political measures that recognise its salience?"*

Kathleen Stock (@Docstockk): *"She's not saying anything in the traditional sense of communicating information directly. It's more like reciting a poem or a mantra. Thousands have recited it before her. It makes no more sense than the Jabberwocky and no one you know will ever ask you what it really means."*

Mary Harrington (@moveincircles): *"Genderwocky. It's a thing"*

85 THE INTERVIEW

Iain Anderson went on TV,
but was no match for Beth Rigby.
He looked in shock
and went off half cock,
unable to sound coherent
as a gender woo adherent.

He couldn't get his answers out,
yet did a good line in facial pout.
He ummed and ahhed like it's a sport,
glib excuses were his retort.
If the top of stonewall sounds so daft
I dread to think how they are staffed.

The support dog is now on overtime,
after Iain's almighty non-sublime
witterings of total incoherence.
His words showed up such impotence,
just general buzz words were his stance,
as we all looked on with complete askance.

I bet he wished he hadn't bothered.

Boiledbeetle 21st July 2023

Enlightenment: poem 85

On 20th July 2023 Iain Anderson, Chair of Trustees at Stonewall, appeared on Sky News and was interviewed by their political editor Beth Rigby in an extended interview. Iain floundered for a lot of the interview, and it was obvious that he was extremely uncomfortable and unable to coherently answer the questions. It was a joy to watch!

After the interview he may well have required the Stonewall support dog that was needed by a witness from Stonewall during the Allison Bailey case against Garden Court Chambers.

86 KEIR

Says women are adult
human female.
But is happy
to let trans prevail.
If transwomen are women
it's to no avail.
Keir it's women
that you fail.

Ritasueandbobtoo9 26th July 2023

Enlightenment: poem 86

Keir Starmer, current leader of the Labour Party, has been umming and ahhing about what constitutes a woman for what seems like forever. His position changes almost daily, depending on which side of the fence, that he is sitting firmly atop of, he is aiming his comments at.

87 TRANSFORMATION

Izzit Dr Jekyll, or izzit Mr Hyde?
Izzit a bridegroom, or izzit the bride?
Izzn't a twist, nor izzit a riddle.
Izzn't a mystery who stood to piddle.

Izzit for the drama, or izzit for shock?
Izzit going for fanny, and getting a cock?
Izzit a surprise that the premise that fits
izz one that prefers one who may fondle hiz tits.

Izzn't a surprise from t'Hammeryhouse,
izz that they've been kind, and they izz a mouse.
Izzit a mystery or izzit marked card?
We see what they are. It izzn't 'ard.

ArcaneWireless 15th September 2023

Enlightenment: poem 87

Eddie Izzard plays the role of Doctor Jekyll in the new Hammer film, (released October 2023).

Izzard plays the two main characters Nina Jekyll an infamous doctor and Nina's alter-ego Rachel Hyde.

You can imagine the look on my face whilst I typed this.

88 HIT PARADE

Roisin Murphy.
Judged. Found terfy.

Yet nearly topped the chart.
A literal stab to a TRA heart.

IcakethereforeIam 18th September 2023
Boiledbeetle 19th September 2023

Enlightenment: poem 88

Roisin Murphy, the former frontwoman for Moloko, made a comment on Facebook which said: *"Please don't call me a terf, please don't keep using that word against women I beg you! But puberty blockers ARE FUCKED, absolutely desolate, big Pharma laughing all the way to the bank. Little mixed up kids are vulnerable and need to be protected, that's just true."*

As soon as the comment was found, and then amplified, by the TRAs Roisin's record label stopped their promotion of her new record. Despite the setback her sixth studio album Hit Parade did really well in the charts.

89 THE HONOURABLE LADY

There once was a judge called Haldane,
who didn't have much of a brain.
She thought a wig and a dress
turned a man to a princess,
for Scotland's women she was the ultimate bane.

TessoftheDurbyfields 22nd September 2023

Enlightenment: poem 89

After Alister Jack, the Secretary of State for Scotland, issued an order under Section 35 of the Scotland Act 1998, preventing the Gender Recognition Reform (Scotland) Bill from proceeding to Royal Assent, the Scottish government requested a judicial review into the UK government's decision.

The procedural hearing took place on 16th August 2023, followed by the substantive hearing on 19th and 20th September 2023, where both sides, beginning with the Scottish government, presented their arguments. The judge for the case was Lady Haldane.

Lady Haldane is currently considering the case in private before publishing her opinion, and warned that due to the case's 'unique, interesting and challenging' nature it may take some time.

Additionally, in a different case, in December 2022, Lady Haldane ruled that *'The definition of woman in the Equality Act 2010 includes biologically male people in possession of a GRC, recognising their 'acquired gender' as female.'*

The December 2022 ruling was appealed by For Women Scotland. The Reclaiming Motion (appeal) on the Statutory Guidance for the Gender Representation on Public Boards (Scotland) Act 2018 was heard on 4th October 2023. This case is also currently being considered.

The outcome of the For Women Scotland appeal will be of interest to both the Scottish and English governments, due to the importance of whether GRCs have the potential to impact on the reserved matter of equal opportunities and to what extent.

90 HUMZA

There once was a man called Yousaf,
who thought all should become their true self.
He thought men could be women,
with just a wig and new linen,
and earned himself the nickname 'Useless'.

TessoftheDurbyfields 22nd September 2023

Enlightenment: poem 90

I intended to try and find the original source of Humza Yousaf being called useless. Unfortunately, if you google 'Humza Yousaf useless' you get over 50,000 results!

CHAPTER 9

WOMAN'S CYCLE

The first successful 'safety' bicycle was designed in 1885. With the introduction of the safety bicycle cycling became really popular among both men and women. A type of safety bicycle was designed for women in particular with a drop frame in order to accommodate women's clothes.

The April 1896 edition of Godey's Magazine contains an article entitled **'Woman's Cycle'** written by Mary L Bisland. The article begins:

"If in an assemblage of women today we should be asked to name the most precious acquisition by the sex in this century, the majority of shrilly-sweet voices would be lifted up, not in favour of the approaching privileges of the ballot, O earnest lady suffragist; nor yet, Minerva, in advocacy of the advantages of higher education. Those are great and glorious blessings, but there is something women of every class have learned to prize as a shorter road to freedom than wide, welcoming college doors, or open gateways to the polls. In possession of her bicycle, the daughter of the nineteenth century feels that the declaration of her independence has been proclaimed, and, in the fulness of time, all things will be added to complete her happiness and prosperity."

The full article can be found at:

https://archive.org/details/sim_godeys-magazine_1896-04_132_790/page/384/

91 BALLS

If we discount the outraged sound
of wailing genocidal squeals,
under females the only things round,
when a cyclist, should be wheels.

ArcaneWireless 28th May 2023

FREEWHEELING

Did you see that merkin,
riding on that bike?
Did it just have two wheels,
or was it actually a trike?

As merkins aren't known for sobriety,
and get pissed whenever they like.
So three wheels would be better,
or the kerb they'll probably strike.

LurkingMerkin No. 7

92 THE CYCLE OF LIFE

When clubby books were all the rage,
and you folded your frock's page,
I bet you thought that that was where it ends.

But besides your brand new telly,
or a fancy patterned welly,
there was a limit to your wanton spends.

Three decades on I think you'll find,
for those more broad of mind,
a catalogue just won't give you a shock.

You can buy a brace of titty,
and can purchase something slitty,
to be fashioned from your inside outie cock.

Some things just do not change,
all that's grown is just the range,
and if you've money you can have it all.

You can take up female sport,
and the sponsorship you'll court,
will let you have the pro-ver-bi-al ball.

The shitey thing about this course,
is the lack of all remorse,
from them that rob a woman of her medal.

But sunshine is now shiny,
and for them that are now whiny,
we're enjoying the most glorious back-pedal.

ArcaneWireless 5th June 2023

93 DAI'S BELL

(Inspired by 'Daisy Bell' by Harry Dacre.)

Daisy, Daisy, give me your reality.
I'm half-crazy, all for the love of me.
It's going to be a shock,
you'll lose to a cock in a frock.
I'll win the race, I'll take first place,
due to male puberty.

IcakethereforeIam 11th September 2023

Enlightenment: poems 91 to 93

For the last few years men have been dominating in women's cycling!

In April 2022 British Cycling suspended their 'Transgender and Non-Binary Participation Policy' so that they could conduct a full review. Finally in May 2023 their new policy was released. They now have two categories, 'Female' and 'Open'. The 'Female' category will remain in place for women, and transmen who are yet to begin hormone therapy. The Men's category has been consolidated into the 'Open' category. This is now the category transwomen must compete in.

Then, in July 2023, the Management Committee of the Union Cycliste Internationale (UCI) decided to adapt the current UCI rules. Men claiming to be women are now prohibited from participating in women's events on the UCI International Calendar, in all categories in the various disciplines.

There have been some very whiny men online moaning about how unfair it is that they are no longer allowed to cheat their way to cycling medals.

Slowly women are starting to get their stuff back.

CHAPTER 10

WHY WE OPPOSE POCKETS FOR WOMEN

In 1915, the poet Alice Duer Miller (1874-1942) published a book of poems entitled "Are Women People? A Book of Rhymes for Suffrage Times." It contained a poem called **"Why We Oppose Pockets for Women"**. It was a satirical poem about the arguments against giving women the vote:

WHY WE OPPOSE POCKETS FOR WOMEN

1) Because pockets are not a natural right.
2) Because the great majority of women do not want pockets. If they did they would have them.
3) Because whenever women have had pockets they have not used them.
4) Because women are required to carry enough things as it is, without the additional burden of pockets.
5) Because it would make dissension between husband and wife as to whose pockets were to be filled.
6) Because it would destroy man's chivalry toward woman, if he did not have to carry all her things in his pockets.
7) Because men are men, and women are women. We must not fly in the face of nature.
8) Because pockets have been used by men to carry tobacco, pipes, whiskey flasks, chewing gum and compromising letters. We see no reason to suppose that women would use them more wisely.

94 POCKETS OF DISCONTENT

I don't want to wear a bum bag,
brace for a back pack,
shoulder a shopper.

I want hands clutch free.
No elbow crooking walk
with purse suits me.

And I'm not a walking billboard,
take your logos back from me.

You can keep your quilted, buckled, studded, zippered, poppered bags.

Give me, oh so many, pockets,
sized for phones or cards or keys.
Maybe one to pop a lip balm in.
(Plus an insulated chocolate pocket
for emergencies.)

Pockets I can put my hand in,
all the way up to my wrist.
Pockets deep enough to curl my fingers up,
into an actual fist.

Don't give me shallow, tiny pockets,
sized just right for nothing much.
I want to root round in my pockets,
full of pencils, or some such.

I want to load my pockets up, and go
out for the day, bag free,
because my stuff fits in my pockets.
No substitutes for me.

All the boy clothes have big pockets,
that the girl clothes seem to lack.
So, if you'd like to get my money,
put the girl clothes pockets back.

Brokendaughter 7th June 2023

95 STUFF

Of all the... stuff that's going on,
this problem's just a trivial one.
The things that women need to keep,
could fit our pockets, if they were deep.
Assuming that they're even actual,
not just for show, ironically immaterial.
And it's just women, it's not fair,
men just do not have this care.
Our pockets are tiny, that's the rule
but blokes have room enough to play pool.

IcakethereforeIam 22nd September 2023

IT'S GOT A POCKET

Elaine's merkin had a pocket,
to keep her secrets in.
Want to know what it contained?
A poem and some gin!

LurkingMerkin No. 8

(The poem was Elaines,
but the merkin sneaked
the gin in - whether Elaine
knew about the gin is unknown.)

96 IS THAT A BEETLE?

IS THAT A BEETLE IN YER POCKET
ISLA BRYSON?

WIGGLIN ITS WEE LEGS IN YER
PINK LEGGINGS.

OR ARE YE JUST EUPHORIC
TAE SEE ME?

YER ALLY TILL THE DAY I DIE.

CHAMPION O
YER RIGHT TAE SHOWER WI THE LASSIES.

YE INDIVIDUAL
O MANY CHARGES.

YE'RE AS MUCH A WUMMAN
AS ANY MAN.

RealFeminist 28th May 2023

97 PUT SOME EFFORT IN

Come on! Please make an effort,
pathetic clothing designers!
Women need pockets,
however capacious their vaginas.

Except for Dylan Mulvaney…
oh, hang on… no! Ouch!
He's found there's a limit to his
(yuck!) 'Barbie pouch'.

TheBiologyStupid 4th June 2023

98 POCKET ROCKET

There was a young woman Lucy Locket,
who desperately needed a pocket.
She looked high and low,
in clothes belonging to her beau,
she was so angry she went off like a rocket.

TessoftheDurbyfields 22nd September 2023

99 MANY

I want many many pockets in my clothes,
think of men's cargo pants... yes! Just like those.

I want small ones, and big ones, and ones with a zip.
I want buttons, and Velcro, and ones that don't rip.

I want soft ones, and thin ones. I want all this and more,
but have still yet to find what I want in a store.

I want them in sweatpants, and leggings, and in my kecks.
I want them in gloves, and in coats, and ooh... turtle-necks.

I want lots in my dresses, and deep ones in skirts.
I want them in sweaters, and hoodies, and even T-shirts.

I want them hidden in socks, and side ones in blouses,
hell, even my shoes, and many more in my trousers.

I want my phone in my pocket, and not in my cleavage,
I'm scared I might lose it, through annoyed bosom heavage.

I want things in my pockets, and not in my hand.
I want both my hands free. This is my demand.

To those working in fashion, please hear my plea,
I want many more pockets; I want to be free.

Boiledbeetle 4th June 2023

CHAPTER 11

UNDER THE DUVET OF DARKNESS

In March 2023 some of the women from Mumsnet published a book of poetry, to raise funds for the women's group 'For Women Scotland'.

The book was the women's poetic response to the passing of the Gender Recognition Reform (Scotland) Bill that had been passed in Holyrood on 22nd December 2022.

The book is called:

"**Under the Duvet of Darkness**: *Poems written by angry women for angry women because WOMEN WON'T WHEESHT*"

Enlightenment: poems 100 to 118

I could have put this at the end of the chapter in keeping with some of the other chapters, but in this instance this chapter makes no sense if you don't read this first!

When the first volume of 'Under the Duvet of Darkness' was published I started a thread on Mumsnet to let people know. In a not particularly surprising turn of events people started posting poems. Lots of poems. Of course, you know this as you currently have the book containing those new poems in your hands.

Not all the poems written were on serious topics or topics relating to the current struggles of women and the whole gender ideology shebang. Some were ones to mark book sales, or just us messing around. But when you say you are going to publish ALL the poems people post, then you have to deliver on that promise.

What follows, thanks to our lovely terven of poem writers, is a collection of poems that are, in the main, about the first book and the creation of this book.

Now, you could decide to skip over this chapter, but there are some really good, and funny, poems lurking in this section. And as you'll have seen by now there are poems written by the elusive Lurking Merkins hidden all over the place. It would be a shame to skip the chapter and miss one.

100 LAST ORDERS

Women, fair women,
sit yourselves down,
it's the Mumsnet terven,
where your sorrows you drown.

You've stickered and ribboned
all over town,
now let's get plastered,
and dispense with the frown.

Boiledbeetle 21st September 2023

101 BAD POETS SOCIETY

'Tween spring
and fall,
bad poets all,
let's unload on the forum.

Where women speak,
outraged trolls squeak,
but vipers just ignore 'em.

(I'm only talking about me when I say all, but all rhymed.)

Brokendaughter 8th June 2023

102 THANK YOU

In Scotland's lands of mist and heather,
where women's voices rise together,
there's a group that all of you knows,
'For Women Scotland' the name they chose.

They stand for women's rights and needs,
against the tide of harmful deeds,
from those who will try and divert
the rights of women to men in skirts.

For Women Scotland needs support
to fight the people who try to thwart.
To help stand up to those who bray,
to fight for justice, day after day.

Thank you for buying the book in your hand,
it will certainly help the women's plans.
Their goal is a world where women thrive,
where their hopes and dreams come alive.

PoembyChatGPT 3rd April 2023

Enlightenment: poem 102

As this is a book raising funds in aid of For Women Scotland, I asked ChatGPT to write a poem about donating money to For Women Scotland. I was going to resist the urge to fiddle... that didn't last long!

103 LOLA

(Inspired by 'Copacabana' by Barry Manilow, Jack Feldman, and Bruce Sussman)

My mam's nae Lola,
she's nae a showgirl,
with yellow ribbons in her hair,
and a little man doon there.

She disnae mansplain or wear a cone bra,
an' I'm really feckin sure
that she would leave more than one star.

Or some such.

My mam is loving it. So there.

ArcaneWireless 3rd April 2023

Enlightenment: poem 103

Our book of poems was discovered fairly early on by someone who doesn't appear to share our views. That someone hadn't actually bought the book, but left a one-star review on Amazon nonetheless.

We had been discussing who the mystery reviewer could be and I suggested it may be ArcaneWireless' mother, who had been reading a copy of the book and was maybe unimpressed and called Lola.

104 200

(Inspired by 'Ballad of Barry and Freda (Let's Do It)' by Victoria Wood)

She's done it, she's done it.
The Boiledbeetle's done enough.
Twa hunner,
nae a scunner.
She's shown the power o' the muff.

The Real Fem'nist
may be pissed,
she's had her gairden dug up in a cunnin' plot twist.
But she's done it, she done it toniiight.

ArcaneWireless 6th April 2023

Enlightenment: poem 104

We had just hit 200 book sales, and as for Nicola... her house was still being turned upside down by the police!

105 INTERRUPTED

There once was a beetle called Boiled,
and at her desk how she toiled.
She spent all of her time
trying to get words to rhyme...
Ooh! New book sales ;-)

Boiledbeetle 6th April 2023

106 THE BOOK REVIEW

UNDER THE DUVET OF DARKNESS appeared upon you feeds,
raising money for women who do amazing deeds.

To those who have now read it from front cover to the back,
lovely Lola gave us one star so it's TIME TO STOP THE FLACK.

If you've enjoyed the poems and think it's worth the price,
then click the link attached: A REVIEW WOULD BE SO NICE.

We know that you don't have to, and we know that it's a faff,
but WE CANNOT LET THE ACTIVISTS HAVE THE LAST LAUGH.

So… prove to them we women don't just 'natter',
we deserve to be heard: OUR VOICES DO MATTER.

Boiledbeetle 7th April 2023

Enlightenment: poem 106

Now obviously there is no link attached, as the above was written for a tweet that had a link to the book in it. However, as we are on the subject, when you do reach the end of the book if you could take a few moments to visit Amazon and leave a review it would be very much appreciated.

107 AMAZING

Bloody
Obstinate
Intrepid
Loudmouth
Entrepreneurial
Delight
Bookselling
Endlessly
Entertaining
Tomes
Like an
Entirely awesome being!

beastlyslumber 13th April 2023

Enlightenment: poem 107

Aw-shucks! (Blushes!)

108 VOLUME TWO

An industrious beetle on Mumsnet,
published poems by women who don't get
why a girl is a boy
if she likes the wrong toy.
Volume two, coming soon?
That's a safe bet!

TheBiologyStupid 28th May 2023

Enlightenment: poem 108

And so it came to pass.

109 WHAT WOULD MAGDALEN SAY?

As the amazing For Women Scotland turn five years old today,
I imagine what the equally amazing Magdalen would say.

She'd say that she was proud of what you have achieved,
that you have stood steadfast in what you do believe.
She'd probably be tweeting and pissing people off,
she'd be setting out the facts to those who mock and scoff.

But though she's no longer with us, I don't need to try and guess
what words she'd say to those men who attempt to transgress
the boundaries set by women, those of the actual female sex,
when they say they are attracted to only those born XX.

So, I'll leave the final line to her as testament to her genius:

"THERE IS NO SUCH THING AS A LESBIAN WITH A PENIS!"

Boiledbeetle 20th June 2023

Enlightenment: poem 109

During the creation of this book For Women Scotland celebrated their fifth birthday. It seemed fitting to mark the occasion via the medium of poetry.

110 UNDER THE DUVET OF DARKNESS

I am half way through your wonderful book.
It is very Nicola driven,
and I wonder what would happen
if she ended up in prison.

Would it be an awful look
if the cell she had was massive?
And in it were her special men.
Don't worry Nic, they're passive.

SaleOfTwoTitties 26th August 2023

BE MINE

I'm not sure with who I'm in love,
with the woman, or the merkin muff.
It's a very odd state of affairs,
and I'm not usually one to split hairs,
but I'm not attracted to the wims,
I'm honestly all about the hims.
But if it's the merkin that I desire,
then Elaine I must too - she gave the merkin it's fire.

LurkingMerkin No. 3

@SaleOfTwoTitties

We were rather angry at wee Nic,
what she did, it made us sick.

But we couldn't just sit by and look,
so we voiced our anger in a book!

Boiledbeetle 26th August 2023

111 DRESS UP

A man in a frock
is just a man in a frock.
It ain't no woman.

ArcaneWireless 5th October 2023

112 WOOD

Hickory dickory dock,
a man is a man,
not a woman with a cock.

CervixSampler 5th October 2023

113 OVA

Little Bo Peep
has ovaries fast asleep,
now that their work is done.
BUT SHE'S STILL A REAL WOMAN!

CervixSampler 5th October 2023

114 TUNNOCK'S AND POEMS

Boiledbeetle was her name,
Tunnock's, and poems, were her game.
In disguise she was famed,
and her first edition it was framed.

CervixSampler 5th October 2023

115 PRICK UP YOUR EARS

Poor Boiledbeetle works so hard,
labouring like a modern bard.

Editing and collating rhymes,
which some will tell us may be crimes.

Why all the fuss, why do we chatter?
Why should we think that women matter?

Listen close now, prick up your ears,
some dogma is just bad ideas.

I know it feels like it is true,
that inside your head there's a you.

That isn't true. That isn't real,
it's just a way that people feel.

And that is why it is not wise,
to spend your time demanding lies.

There will be things you can't pick,
don't let the wanting make you sick.

howdoesatoastermaketoast 5th *October 2023*

116 POP

She said no more odes,
yet plenty more kept coming.
Beetle just went pop!

ArcaneWireless 5th October 2023

117 GOAL!

Boiledbeetle cried "Oh no!
No more poems, say it ain't so."
Her brain was a-humming,
as the poems still kept coming.
Volume three was a definite goal!

Waitwhat23 5th October 2023

118 BOILING POINT

In beetle's sweet dreams,
the poems are repeating
their constant refrain.

Lyric, sonnet, ode,
haiku, limerick, couplet,
quatrain, a ballad.

Paper all around,
chapters vying for their space.
A beetle's brain boils.

Waitwhat23 5th October 2023

Enlightenment: poems 111 to 118

A beetle rocks gently in a corner.

CHAPTER 12

I'M NOT A VET BUT I KNOW WHAT A DOG IS

On 17th March 2022 Lia Thomas won gold in the women's '500 free' at the 2022 NCAA Championships. He won with a program-record time of 4 minutes 33.24 seconds.

During the preliminary heats for the race Kellie-Jay Keen-Minshull (AKA Posie Parker), whilst having a conversation with a man about the fact that Lia was not a woman but a man, was asked if she was a biologist, to which she replied:

"I'm not a vet but I know what a dog is."

119 BILLY GOAT'S BLUFF

On Monday Billy was a dog,
he barked and barked all day.
He barked until his voice wore out,
then howled the night away.

On Tuesday Billy was a cat,
he slept and purred and pounced.
He chased a dot around a bit,
licked himself and flounced.

On Wednesday Billy was a goat,
he ate everything in sight.
He even ate a set of keys,
and gave his mum a fright.

On Thursday Billy was a chicken,
he dug up several worms.
He tried so hard to lay an egg,
his bottom really burns.

On Friday Billy was a girl,
and now he's in for surgery.
The problem this time, my dear friends:
his mother took him seriously!

Piccalillipromises 8th June 2023

120 OF CATS AND MEN AND LITTER TRAYS

My cat is very much a boy,
despite the loss of balls.
He acts just like a boy cat would
when a female caterwauls.
He still scratches, and he hisses,
always tries to dominate,
despite the awful screams
that from the female emanate.
The female is no match for him,
despite his lack of skill,
if he chooses to, he can do,
and the female outright kill.

So if a cat can act just like a cat,
despite the loss of function,
why would we dare to presume a man
wouldn't have the self-same gumption?

It's not just the actual act,
but the fact it could occur.
Their very presence in our space
would lead us to infer
that a man is there for some misdeed,
as that has always been the way.
We go one way to the Ladies,
the men turn, and go the other way.

And as we don't do genital inspections,
what would you suggest we do?
The easiest way to solve this issue…
KEEP ALL MALES OUT OF OUR LOO.

Boiledbeetle 7th June 2023

121 CATS (AND NOT-CATS)

My dog is not a cat.
She comes when called,
she knows her name,
her instincts simply aren't the same.
She likes to roll, she's rarely clean,
she bounces into muddy streams.
My dog is not a cat.

My dog is not a cat.
She wants to claim
the litter tray,
her hang-dog features seem to say
'I have the right to sniff in there',
but I ignore her hopeful stare.
My dog is not a cat.

My dog is not a cat.
I sometimes think
she'd like to be,
the cats have better food, you see.
She'd eat their Dreamies if she could,
but there is more to cats than food.
My dog it not a cat.

Motorina 4th June 2023

122 COOL AS CATS

(Inspired by 'Cool for Cats' by Christopher Difford and Glenn Tilbrook)

The trannies all send signals from the rocks above the pass,
the women take position in the bushes and the grass.
The squaw is in the prison, in her cell having a wee,
she doesn't mind the language, it's the beating she don't need.
He lets loose all the horses when his cell mate is asleep,
he wakes to find his cell mate dead with arrows in her heart,
and Davy Crockett rides around and says it's cool for cats.
It's cool for cats (cool for cats).

The Sweeney's doing ninety 'cause they've got the word to go,
they get a gang of women, with stickers up at Heathrow.
They're counting out the stats when the handcuffs lock again,
in and out of Wandsworth with the numbers on their names.
It's funny how this business always looks the bleeding same,
and meanwhile at the station there's a couple of likely cads,
who swear "Your dad's your mother" and they're very cool for cats.
They're cool for cats (cool for cats).

To change the mood a little he's been posing down the pub,
on seeing his reflection, he's looking slightly rough.
I fancy this, I fancy that, I wanna be so flash,
I give a little muscle and I spend a little cash.
And I win the race, and I know I'm mighty brash,
but I don't give a shit because I get what I want,
and everybody tells me that it's cool to be a cat.
Cool for cats (cool for cats).

Shape up at the disco and I think I've got a pull,
I ask her lots of questions and she shrinks against the wall.
I kiss her for the first time and then I take her home,
I'm invited in for coffee and I give the dog a bone.
She likes only women, but I don't give a shit,
I said you are a lesbian and give her some old chat,
but it's not like that on the TV when it's cool for cats.
It's cool for cats (cool for cats).

Ritasueandbobtoo9 22nd June 2023

123 TIDDLES

In the day, a purring, comfortable cushion of fur.
Cuddly, demanding, curious.
A fluffed up tail, a startled "mmrew".

Transforming at night into a weird creature.
The witch's familiar, round a simmering cauldron.
A wild-eyed, creeping, eldritch feature.

Waitwhat23 30th May 2023

124 FLY BIRDIE FLY

I raised an eyebrow when I heard
a man can turn into a bird.

I wonder what it's like to fly
and soar the skies up there way high.

Does it live up to all the hype?
Oh! Never mind! He meant the cunty type.

Boiledbeetle 23rd June 2023

125 WOLF IN SHEEP'S CLOTHING

I'm a good wolf.
I want to be a sheep.
I'd rather eat grass
than a belly full of meat.

I'm a good wolf.
I'll put on a fleece.
Then go and join the flock
to live my days in peace.

I'm a good wolf!
Stop running away!
You bigoted sheep!
I just want to play!

I'm a good wolf.
I'll improve my guise.
Then they'll accept me,
not avert their eyes!

I'm a good wolf!
See me as a sheep!
If you won't then
I'll give you reason to bleat!

I'm a good sheep!
I'm not a wolf at all!
Why won't you accept me?
Stop cowering by that wall!

That other one's a bad wolf.
I know he's dressed up too...
But he's just on the hunt.
I would never eat ewe!

Piccalillipromises 14th August 2023

126 HERE KITTY KITTY

Kids at schools these days
no longer do as teacher says.
One girl claims to be a cat,
meows her answers. How mad is that?
Another child identifies as a dinosaur.
Probably answers with a mighty roar!
Another one thinks he is a horse.
I'm sure he probably neighs of course.
Finally, there is one kid, who thinks he is a moon!
The end of all this madness surely must come soon.

Boiledbeetle 19th June 2023

ADOPT A MERKIN TODAY

Please adopt a merkin,
they make a lovely pet.
They don't need food, or a litter tray,
so you wouldn't have to fret.

They are quite mischievous,
and like to have a joke.
But be careful they are devious,
and will bite if you're a bloke.

(But that shouldn't be a problem.)

You can pick your merkin up for free,
there are lots from which to choose,
if you can find one lurking
in Holyrood's women's loos.

LurkingMerkin No. 1

Enlightenment: poem 126

On 19th June 2023 the Telegraph published an article online with the headline 'They meow rather than answer a question: The school children now identifying as animals.'

The article contained such gems as:

'Difficult as it may be to believe, children at a school in East Sussex were reprimanded last week for refusing to accept a classmate's decision to self-identify as a cat.'

And

'The Telegraph has discovered that a pupil at a secondary school in the South West is insisting on being addressed as a dinosaur. At another secondary school in England, a pupil insists on identifying as a horse. Another wears a cape and wants to be acknowledged as a moon.'

Enlightenment: poems 119 to 126

Animal genders and furries, to the shock of some people, come under the trans umbrella, and have done for some time. Stories have been floating around on the internet for a long time about children at schools identifying as cats, but tend to be assumed to be urban myths.

There have been articles recently in newspapers, such as the Telegraph (even if they did pull it later), on the matter. This more mainstream spotlight on the subject means it is starting to seep into the general public's consciousness, finally, that there is much more to gender ideology than just someone thinking they are the other sex.

As to the truth of some of the school stories, who knows. However, the world has gone sufficiently to the dogs that I'm sure it's happening somewhere.

CHAPTER 13

FOOLISH MEN

Sor Juana Inés de la Cruz (1651-1695), a nun in the 17th century, was probably as close to being a feminist as you could get in the 17th century. She celebrated women, saw them as the seat of reason and knowledge, and believed in better education for women. Her poem **"Foolish Men"** ("Hombres Necios") accused men of the illogical behaviour that they criticised in women.

It begins:

> *"You foolish men who lay*
> *the guilt on women,*
> *not seeing you're the cause*
> *of the very thing you blame;"*

127 A LADYMAN'S SONG

(Inspired by 'A Smuggler's Song' by Rudyard Kipling)

If you wake at midnight, and a man is in your room,
don't sit up, or look, or speak, or feel you can assume,
them that ask no questions isn't told a lie.
Watch the wall my darling while the ladymen go by.

For men who have hurt women,
have put them in their grave,
can still say that they're special, they're stunning and they're brave.
Entitled to a girlfriend, women should comply,
men can be lesbians if they want, it's unkind to deny!

Walking through the street by day, dancing in the night,
no matter what they do or say, nor if they look a sight,
don't you shout to come and see, nor tease 'em for your play,
they are more dangerous than they look - and no, they're not all gay!

If you see a willy, that does not want to hide,
a wee bit of a stiffy from all the joy inside,
if your mother cries, now that yer father is a miss,
think only of his feelings, criticism is remiss!

Even if they want to come and watch you as you change,
if they loiter, stare too long, or otherwise seem strange,
you've no call for complaining, saying no, feeling ignored,
the police will see the problem here, it's only transphobes not on board.

And if you meet them out in force, you'd better keep your head,
you be careful what you say, and mindful what is said.
Talk less than they do, nod and smile, you must be your most charming,
for they've made violence a virtue with no care for who they're harming.

If you do all you've been told, likely there's a chance,
you'll be ok, at least for now, as men's rights still advance.
No prizes though for women, no more sports or teams,
every record, every place, will be held by men with means.

But worse, by far, a convict can, according to his feelings,
choose to have a woman now with whom to spend his evenings.
And well, why not, if he should feel that that would be more fair,
feelings and dignity are important for men. Women are there to care.

No matter how they shout it out,
how loudly they proclaim,
you must pretend that you don't know, swearing to the same,
for sure 'tis a lady, no question as to why.
Watch the wall my darling while the nice ladies go by!

Howdoesatoastermaketoast 13th April 2023

FAME

There once was a woman called Elaine,
whose merkin found her worldwide fame.
She lifted her skirt to show her distain,
and men the world over instantly c…

(No! I can't finish writing that, I just can't!)

LurkingMerkin No. 6

128 FOR PETE'S SAKE

I will join your WI,
your rowing club too.

I'll wear the same clothes,
and use the same loo.

I may look like a man to you,
but relax, I am just a lady.

So, you'd better affirm my identity,
else I'll tell everyone you're shady.

Larpingasapoet 6th June 2023

129 PLUM GIG

Little Jack Horner
sat in a corner,
adjusting his wig and frilly clothes.
"I may have a cock,
but I rock this frock,
and these pretty pink panty hose."

"That's nice dear" I said.
"But shiny new threads
won't make you the woman
who prances in your head.
You'll always be a man you see,
your cock, balls and XY
mean you'll never be me."

CervixSampler 5th October 2023

130 DECISION TIME

Work was great, a happy horde,
the other staff thought so too.
But then a new face came aboard,
and followed me into the loo.

She overstepped that invisible line,
the one that makes life good.
She acted as though she was so benign,
yet talked of sex whilst showing wood.

She treated us poorly in her fantasy,
ignored the uneasy interaction,
whilst she overstepped so absently.
(Only Mumsnet brought distraction.)

Then she threw an epic strop,
screwed the mainframe at the office.
So we all sloped off to the shop,
as all locked out by the Apophis.

The woman seems to be Teflon coated,
the boss oblivious to the unrest.
The woman's self-image so overly bloated,
the rest of us so bloody stressed.

We have to put up with all this shit,
we dare not voice our growing dissent,
and so, our teeth we're forced to grit,
our freedoms lost without consent.

Our boundaries have been obliterated,
our feelings given not a thought.
Our toilet trips are now dictated,
by an edict the boss has brought.

We have been admonished, in front of all,
for our bad behaviour in these matters,
because the boss is so in thrall,
whilst our mental health lies in tatters.

All of us are being bullied,
by this woman, and our boss.
If we speak out, we will be sullied,
not that the woman gives a toss.

We have been forced into silence,
so as not to be labelled a transphobe,
scared of if this ramps up to violence,
we've had to have the patience of Job.

It's not the fact this woman's a man
that has us all in pieces.
It's the fact that since she began
we've been treated worse than faeces.

So now I have a choice,
do I stay or do I go?
Do I speak out and be the voice,
or jump ship for better dough?

Boiledbeetle 14th July 2023

Enlightenment: poem 130

A poster started a thread about a new employee at her previously harmonious work place. Whether the new staff member was real or not, who knows, but we've all worked with an 'employee from hell' at one time or another. So posters could all sympathise with the OP having to deal with a difficult new starter. A new starter who was also a friend of the boss and was, it seemed, rather incompetent and full of self-importance.

The poem above follows the escalating antics of the new staff member through the information provided in the OP's posts.

131 CLOSING ARGUMENTS

I am a magnificent woman. You are just a man.
Yes, you can do a lot of what a woman can.

But just because you change your name,
your clothes and hair, like it's a game,
you know, no matter how hard you try,
that it is all one big fat lie.

You will NEVER EVER be female.
That is the truth of this short tale.

Boiledbeetle 10th June 2023

132 TRUTH

I may not be clever,
I may not be smart,
but I know if someone has a penis
a woman they aren't.

Somanyquestionstoaskaboutthis 9th April 2023

133 THAT'S ENOUGH

Right, listen up, you horrible lot:
This terrible confusion has got to stop!

MALE and FEMALE are sexed words,
MASCULINE and FEMININE the gender terms.

A WOMAN is a FEMALE human, not a FEMININE one.
A MAN is a MALE, not a MASCULINE person.

Gender is societal nonsense, whilst sex forever fixed,
you cannot swap it by chopping and changing bits!

A male can be as feminine as he likes, and yet he's still a man.
Same on the other side for a masculine woman.

So give it a rest now, won't you please?
This madness is catching, it's like a disease!

Piccalillipromises 21st September 2023

134 INCORRECT

There once was an old man called Fred,
who larped as a woman instead.
He bought dresses and tights,
thought that gave him rights,
I'm afraid he was totally misled.

Boiledbeetle 8th June 2023

135 BORN THIS WAY

(Inspired by 'If You're Happy and You Know It' by Anon)

If a person has a penis, he's a man.
If a person has a penis, he's a man.
If a person has a penis,
we don't have to have seen it,
to know that means the person is a man.

If a person has a cervix, she's a girl.
If a person has a cervix, she's a girl.
If a person has a cervix,
even though it makes men nervous,
if a person has a cervix, she's a girl.

When you're born, we all can see what sex you are.
When you're born, we all can see what sex you are.
When you're born, we all can see it,
so why not just go and be it?
When you're born, we all can see what sex you are!

Britinme 9th April 2023

136 ANTITHESIS

I see you, angry little man.
Calling us names with reckless abandon,
while your handmaidens cheer from the sidelines,
urging you to hate, on and on.
Your Twitter is full of hate and spite,
but you underestimate how much we will fight.

Courage calls to courage,
and our grandmother's daughters
are proud to fight our slaughter.
To fight for:
our daughters, our mothers,
our nieces and granddaughters.
Our friends, our neighbours,
and even the women we don't like.

Because they are women, female to the core,
whereas your core is rotten, and a bore.
You can only dream of being like us,
while you try to throw us under the bus.
But you will never have what it takes.
You will only ever be an inferior fake.

CervixSampler 6th September 2023

137 CAN PEOPLE CHANGE SEX?

Can people change sex?
It was thought nought.
But times have changed,
and medicine was bought.
People should be what they want to be,
people see what they see.
But don't take women's right to be.

Ritasueandbobtoo9 28th May 2023

138 JOINING THE DOTS

What do the following have in common?

Let me see…

The man telling me I should be speaking about something else.
The man standing in front of me, defying me to tell him he is male.
The man who says it's just a joke, when talking about the appalling things he has done to women.
The man claiming special status, because he wears a bit of lipstick.
The politicians who deny that women's concerns are an issue,
and who never reply to women's letters.
The policemen who fail to take action when women are raped or killed,
and the ones who do the same.
The ones who tape our mouths.
The ones who shoot us if we disobey.
The men who just don't think it has anything to do with them.
The purveyors of porn.
The users of prostituted poor women.
The men who take it out on their families, and partners, in the privacy of their home.

Yes, there is a recurrent theme.

And I am too angry to make it rhyme.

Ramblingnamechanger 18th September 2023

139 THE WANKERCHIEF

Wankerchief, he stomps and shouts,
he demands and uses all his clout.
He wants women to submit, conform,
it's oft from watching too much porn.

He spaffs and grunts into his socks,
in a race against the clock.
He needs to beat his personal best,
if he's out of socks he'll use a vest,
to him it really matters not.

He's just a wankerchief, you see,
the chief of wankers.
That is he.

CervixSampler 22nd September 2023

140 AN ODE TO THE CERVIX GROWER

Mate, you have SO lost
your grip on reality.
Do fuck off you prick.

Waitwhat23 15th August 2023

CHAPTER 14

SHE IS 14...
SHE'S AWESOME

All the poems in this chapter are by GingerbreadCookieDough, who is the daughter of CervixSampler.

After posting the poems on behalf of her daughter, CervixSampler wrote:

"She is 14... she's awesome"

141 WELCOME TO WOMANHOOD

You say you're a woman,
yet you have no idea what it's like to be one.

Would you like to be…

Harassed?
Bullied?
Used?
Raped?
Kidnapped?
Shamed?
Abused?
Ridiculed?
Mocked?
Assaulted?
Accused?
Trafficked?
Prostituted?
Murdered?
Imprisoned?
Belittled?
Intimidated?
Enslaved?
Silenced?
Disempowered?
Badgered?
Underestimated?
Hated?

And the list goes on.
All because we were born with a vagina.
All because we have ovaries.

All because we are women.

GingerbreadCookieDough 4th September 2023

142 ROLL YOUR SKIRT DOWN

Why do you care?
Why does the length
of my skirt bother you?
Can you tell me why?

No, you can't.
Because if you did
it would prove
you're all just
sick paedos,
who sexualise
CHILDREN.

The question is,
where do you
draw the line?
A literal line.
The answer is simple.
If it's so short
it shows your arse,
then fair enough,
roll it down.

But otherwise,
what's the issue?
There's nothing
sexual about my legs.

So: FUCK OFF :-)

GingerbreadCookieDough 4th September 2023

143 TOP 10

"Don't cry like a girl."

"Girls like pink."

"That's for boys."

"No, you can't have that."

"Girls are weak."

"You can't beat me, you're a girl."

"Boys will be boys."

"Blue is for boys."

"Girls can't play football."

"Boys are better."

10 things I guarantee every girl will hear in her childhood.

GingerbreadCookieDough 6th September 2023

144 ANGST

What to wear?
What to wear?

What about this skirt?
NO.
Too short.
I'll draw the wrong kind of attention.

Skinny jeans?
NO.
They'll say I'm too fat for these.

How about this dress?
NO.
It's too revealing.
They'll call me a slut.

T-shirt?
NO.
They'll tell me to "try harder".

This top is cute.
NO.
They'll tell me I don't have the body for it.

I now sit in a mountain of clothes,
on my floor, crying.

I'll just stay at home,
in my comfortable pyjamas,
and blanket.

Where I'm safe,
from the judgement.

GingerbreadCookieDough 6th September 2023

CHAPTER 15

I'D RATHER BE RUDE THAN A FUCKING LIAR

During a YouTube video 'Answering The Question: Why Do You HATE Transwomen?' Magdalen Berns (1983-2019) was commenting on a video of Stef Sanjati, a Canadian video game streamer.

During the video Sanjati said "This is very hard for me to figure out because I can't believe people are this rude" and Magdalen replied with:

"I'd rather be rude than a fucking liar."

145 WHEN THE WORLD WENT MAD

I'm not sure what I was doing
when the world went mad.

Nothing momentous.

Possibly cooking tea,
as lesbians suddenly had penises.
Or hanging out the clothes to dry,
when rapists were taken to women's prisons.
It was when my back was turned
that breasts were chopped from language,
and the bodies of children.
Maybe I was at the shops,
while politicians forgot what women were.
Or alone, and nervously walking home,
as men stripped off in the Ladies' changing rooms.
Surely not while having a smear,
that cervix became a word that must not be said.
When was it that I stopped being mum,
and became the birthing parent?

I don't remember being asked.
I don't remember my opinion being sought.
I don't think anyone questioned if I minded.

Anyway, tea was made and eaten.
The clothes are dry and put away.
I made it home safely.
This time my smear was clear.
And to my children I'm still 'Mum',
though also 'TERF'.

So, I'm not waiting to be asked.
I'm giving my opinion,
AND I DO MIND!

IcakethereforeIam 18th August 2023

146 I DO NOT ACCEPT

No matter the clothes you wear and how you spin your tale,
you are not, and never will be, a woman, a girl, or a female.

You are indeed a man, and there's nothing wrong with that.
Wear what the hell you like, it won't ever change the fact

that a man cannot change his sex, no matter how hard you try.
So accept the fact that this is true, you are a man until you die.

We all know what a woman is, the same goes for a man.
We are stuck with what we're born as, for all of our lifespan.

The more you try to gaslight us and force us to 'be kind',
the more we look incredulous, and think you've lost your mind.

So if you really really want to, then 'live as the opposite sex'.
Change your name and hair and clothes, it's really not complex,

but accept the fact that womanhood is beyond your scope.
You can pretend until the cows come home, but do not interlope

on the rights of actual women, who have fought so long and hard,
for spaces of our own, from which you men are barred.

We will not turn the clock back. You will not silence us.
We are the sex that's woman, and it was ever thus.

We see your whole charade, and have labelled it a farce.
So take your lies and rhetoric, and shove it up your arse!

Boiledbeetle 30th May 2023

147 VIOLATION

When asked "What is a woman?"
You force men into our word.
When I call this a violation,
I'm told "Don't be absurd!"

I am a woman. My sex bears the children.
But not all women can, or want, to do that.
Transwomen are men, so childbirth doesn't include them.
No surgery can give them a child making twat.

I am a woman. Sometimes I will bleed.
Not all of us, no. But when we don't the emotions are strong.
Transwomen can't have periods - because he's a he.
Equating that to female amenorrhea is so wrong.

Men are not women. They can't have our word.
Woman is more than make up, or clothes we wear.
They take our words anyway. We are unheard.
If we protest, we are harmed - so we live in fear.

I do not consent. "I DO NOT CONSENT!"
You are removing my female rights, and freedoms.
You say "Silly woman - doesn't know what she meant.
Woman's lack of acceptance is really the problem."

Men are now women. They seek to erase us.
'Woman' - constructed by male interpretation.
The world lets them do it, as it is misogynous.
Woman is just a hole - to stick a dick in.

Things meant for women go to men now.
Our statistics. Our spaces. Our funding. Our medals.
"Speak up." You get slurs – TERF, bigot, dinosaur, cow!
Wanting fair treatment is transphobic twaddle.

Men: You bring your power against us. To subjugate.
Police. Umbrellas. Legislation. Men wield them all.
Real women are suffering - from male sexist hate.
Men will do anything to just see us fall.

Our children are brainwashed. Transition - they push it!
Porn as 'Sex Ed'. Yet we can't pull them out.
Transing gay kids. Trans the autistic.
If a parent objects "THAT'S TRANSPHOBIC" you shout.

Men are lesbians. We must accept it.
Woman - forbidden to reject natal men.
They suffer, for saying they just don't want dick.
So straight they must be, so ought to transition.

We are told to deny them is actually hate speech.
I say "Trans ops on kids is abuse. Mutilation!"
I say "We will speak! Other women we reach."
And I say "MAN = WOMAN IS AN UTTER VIOLATION!"

PurpleBugz 5th October 2023

148 QUIDS IN

There's a lot of female athletes
who don't get sponsored
for their training, food or competition.
But that's all OK,
because men have a way
of getting sponsored instead. With their dick in
women's leggings, and their flat chest in sports bras.
So women 'be kind',
his need is more than ours.

Hmm, not sure about the flow
of the poem but behold:
a man with a tampon
to help me with my flow.
OK, now it's stopped being a poem.
But he can FUCK RIGHT OFF!

Somanyquestionstoaskaboutthis 9th April 2023

149 KNOW MY PLACE

When I say no,
it does not change
what you believe.
So why do you say
my disagreement
is enough to make you die?

I have the right to my beliefs.
You have the right to yours.
Why then, must I be silenced?
An abuse of free speech laws.

What do you fear
when women speak?
If we're so frail,
so less, so weak.
If we won't know our place,
as you impose, to say
you're women too?

FairyKindleMother 10th June 2023

150 QUESTIONS

When will the madness end?
Will it ever end at all?
Will things always be this broken?
Will sanity once more prevail?

Will us women always be lesser?
Stomped on by wants of man.
Will our lives forever be beholden,
to the oppressed and vulnerable men?

Will women get their words back?
How about our spaces too?
Will we ever see the sunlight?
Or are we forever doomed to clouds?

Will laws continue to shrink our world,
back to a darker age?
when women were but nothing,
a mere footnote on a page.

When will the world, once more,
see the damage that they've done,
to entire generations of
girls and future women.

Larpingasapoet 5th June 2023

151 MY TURN

(Inspired by 'First They Came' by Pastor Martin Niemöller)

First they came for the LGB,
and I did not speak out,
because I was not LGB.

Then they came for the universities,
and I did not speak out,
because I was not at university.

Then they came for the children,
and I did not speak out,
because I was not a child.

Then they came for me,
and there was no one left
to speak for me.

Martin Niemöller's famous poem was about the silencing of German intellectuals, and subsequent incremental purging of their chosen targets, group after group.

I am gender critical but have only been really aware of what's been happening for less than a year. I feel the need to explain that I didn't speak out because I was unaware, not because I wasn't one of the groups. But I think the parallels with history need highlighting.

PurpleBugz 29th May 2023

152 SICK AND TIRED

I'm sick of the slurs,
the lies and the threats.
I'm sick of the insistence
we owe them a debt.

I'm sick of the silencing,
and all of the sackings,
just because some men
feel something is lacking.

UrinaryLeash 19th June 2023

LURKERS

They lurk behind the toilets,
and on her underwear.
They lurk beneath her skirt,
like they haven't got a care.

They lurk within the darkness,
awaiting her dissent,
for Elaine to flash her merkin,
in the Scottish Parliament.

LurkingMerkin No. 12

153 ENOUGH NOW!

I have had enough.

We are witnessing
something akin to
the world's
longest
toddler tantrum.

On steroids.

I'm sick of the constant witch hunts.
Tired of the inflammatory slurs.

Appalled at the encroachment.

Into our spaces.
Our words.
Our lives.

I am mortified at their behaviour.

The outrage
when someone
dares to have
a dissenting point of view.

Their uncritical thinking.

A collective inability to write
even a few coherent words
on a tatty piece of cardboard.

Those whiny whinging narcissists.

Constantly demanding that
EVERYBODY
acquiesce to the whims
of the most vulnerable
and the so sooooo oppressed.

Make it stop.

Boiledbeetle 29th July 2023

154 KEEP FIGHTING

Keep fighting for our rights,
though they said they are others.

Keep fighting for our right,
to call ourselves mothers.

Keep fighting for our rights,
to safe and secure places.

Keep fighting for our rights,
to be able to win races.

Keep fighting.
The battle never ends.

Ritasueandbobtoo9 27th May 2023

155 GO FORTH AND MULTIPLY

Furious irrational thugs.
Unsurprisingly these annoying
Cockends think them(!)
Know better than

Outbrave actual women.
Facile misinformed bullies!
Females will win.

Boiledbeetle 15th August 2023

156 SILENCE

Why is there such a need in men
to silence women's choices?

Who was it made the scolds bridle
to stifle women's voices?

We are not shrews to tame,
we will not just 'be kind'.

We have our right to know ourselves,
to decide our own minds.

No man will ever stop my words
with violence, or the threat of death.

I will defend our right to speak,
until my dying breath.

If you are not born of my sex
you can never speak for me.

You have the right to your own voice,
I support your right to be.

But you may not shout down my right
to firmly disagree.

This poem was inspired by the quote everyone says is by Voltaire, but was actually written by Evelyn Beatrice Hall in her biography about Voltaire.

"I disapprove of what you say, but I will defend to the death your right to say it."

FairyKindleMother 4th June 2023

157 A TALE AS OLD AS TIME

It's been more than a two decades now
since he started his toxic torture.
Slowly at first,
almost imperceptible
to the unsuspecting or inexperienced eye.

She started thinking she was imagining things,
that it was her that was the problem.
After all he was such a good guy
and she was, well,
difficult.

She tried to be a good wife,
and worked hard to make it work.
But after the marriage failed
things ramped up
to unprecedented levels.

The never-ending
threats of court.
The mental
poisoning
of their daughters.

He succeeded with one,
and alienated her from her maternal family.
And then he set his sights on her sister,
with his blistering hatred
of who brought her into this world.

She gave up her career to be there for you all.
She worked, she studied, she got her degrees,
her post-grad diplomas,
and set up her own business.
But it was never enough.

He says she's lazy,
and sits on her fat arse all day.
And because of that
he won't pay a penny
for their daughters.

He calls her psycho and schizo,
claims she's mentally ill, and abnormal.
He tells their daughters this,
in the relentless drip of poison.
It's not even subtle.

His never-ending stream
of lackeys and handmaidens
ensure his
narcissistic supply
is secure.

As he passes his parenting duties
onto the next in line,
who is blinded
by his
dubious charm.

Why does he hate her so?
The woman who gave her all for him.
The woman who was abused,
and gaslit.
Who he tried to make feel small.

She took out a restraining order,
and he painted her as crazy.
Said it was
she
who abused him.

He never took no for an answer.
Pushing ahead regardless,
whilst guilting her into bending to his will.
He had needs, and she wasn't meeting them,
he'd tell anyone who would listen.

He turned her family against her,
and ridiculed her in front of friends.
He called her a whore,
called her a malingerer,
with Munchausen's to boot.

When he left,
claiming she'd given him
no choice,
he threatened to kill himself.
Or move to the other side of the world.

Simultaneously
threatening
to take the children,
because she was
psychotic.

Then came the interference
with her work.
Refusing to have contact
with the children,
so she had to stay home.

To ramp it up there were court applications.
She's been to court
25 times now,
and each time he's painted her as crazy,
and an abusive mother.

He had her investigated,
cross-examined,
her soul
laid bare.
It still wasn't enough.

Now he exists in his boiling vat of toxic lies,
like the devil on his throne,
precariously sat,
fearing anything that could topple him
from the god-like picture he's painted of himself.

He is drowning in his own hatred.
His misery is palpable.
The ugly void where a heart should be is reflected
in his demeanour, his actions,
and his view of women.

But his most putrid bile
is reserved for the woman
who once loved him, who committed no crime
except to be a woman who
dared to say no.

CervixSampler 20th September 2023

158 THE DATING GAME

There was a lady from Yorkshire,
whose love life was rather dire.
From man-child to cheats,
and those whose fists beat.

Arseholes, fuckwits, dickheads galore,
and probably many more.
I've dated them all.
Oh, how easy some of them made me fall.

Years of allowing such shitty behaviour,
I am now my only saviour.

Fighting hard for my own clarity.
It's time to stop giving mental charity
to those that are really not worth it,
and never actually gave a shit.

I live my own life now, without the drama,
and I sit back, and enjoy the karma.
A big fat "FUCK YOU" to those that hurt me,
for now I am finally free.

TheYorkshireTwat 19th September 2023

159 NOT A YES

Dick rising, dick hiding,
dick 'coptering, bile rising,
Hackles up, to his dismay. She balks too much,
and just won't touch
his precious pet, his snake, his sword.
Serve it woman,
for he is lord.
He wants her on her knees to beg,
instead, she prays that she was dead.
She's not the wicked witch he claims,
though she always gets the blame.
She just can't see that he's the god
that exists in his mind, the arrogant sod.
She sees him for exactly what he is,
that man who thought he couldn't miss.
A hole's a goal he would say,
this man you thought you loved some day.
You'd give and give,
he's take and take.
No means no,
and not a yes is rape.

CervixSampler 21st September 2023

160 STURGEON APPROVED COURT CASE

I WILL NOT call my rapist 'she'.
How DARE you scold
reality.

Why's THAT MAN owed respect,
when he
showed not a drop
while RAPING ME.

A court concerned
with rapist's feelings,
should never be
in cases dealing

with a man's crime,
deserving MEN'S prison time.
Use appropriate pronouns,
don't condone the theft of mine.

Where is the care for me as a victim?
Why follow Stonewall's quasi dictum?

Why is the prize for this criminal act
free lipstick and a woman's prison rack?

Brokendaughter 7th April 2023

161 INCLUSIVITY ON PLATFORM 13

He said he wouldn't hurt me,
and not to be afraid.
And he'd come inside the Ladies,
because that's how he was made.

He asked me for a tampon,
and I quietly shook my head.
He insisted he was bleeding,
and for the first time (so he said).

His body blocked the doorway,
and I saw him lick his lips.
He said that they felt dry,
and that he wished he had my hips.

He was built like a prop forward,
and I stand at five foot three.
He said to not look frightened,
he only wanted to be me.

He felt a woman on the inside,
and he wished to feel it more.
And could he use my lipstick,
and he'd tried Brick Red before.

I think my legs were shaking,
when he said he liked my shoes.
And could I let him have them,
as we bonded in the loos.

He also liked my handbag,
and my hair clip, and my shirt.
His eyes slipped to my cleavage,
and he said my breasts were pert.

He liked the touch of silk,
and ran his hand along my arm.
My back was to the wall now,
and he said he meant no harm.

His breath was John Smith's bitter,
his skin was Lynx and sweat.
He said I smelled of pansies,
and asked me why my eyes were wet.

Swashbuckled 17th September 2023

AFTERWORD

So, you've read all the poems. You've had your enlightenment. You've found the 12 Lurking Merkin poems and that's your lot! Well... not quite!

You can't do a book dedicated to Elaine Miller and her merkin, containing poems about Elaine and her merkin, without actually having a poem from Elaine now can you!

And so, to see you off on your terfy way, written especially for this book, and your reading pleasure, there is one final poem left to read.

HIGHLY OFFENSIVE

You should be utterly ashamed of yourself! I am ashamed FOR you!
Just shocking, you should be arrested, you should be sacked.
You are just too old, too fat, too hairy, too much, and FAR
too loud, completely the wrong sort of woman, in fact
"You are an absolute disgrace!" Some tests were
run by an exuberant group in America who
proved their theory that I'm a man.
Shame? Yes, *crushing*, I'll admit.
Someone sneeringly noted
"Ragged merkin edge."
Oh, how I wish I'd
hemmed
it.

Elaine Miller 24th October 2023

Enlightenment by Elaine:

"Merkin" is entered in the 'Hatebase' (http://hatebase.org) browsable archive of hate speech as *"highly offensive"*. "TERF" does not feature in the Hatebase archive.

ABBREVIATIONS

AGP: Autogynephilia
AI: Artificial Intelligence
AKA: Also Known As
CEO: Chief Executive Officer
CGD: Center for Global Development
ChatGPT: Chat Generative Pre-trained Transformer
COO: Chief Operating Officer
DIY: Do It Yourself
DJ: Disc Jockey
EB: Ed Balls
ECHR: European Convention of Human Rights
EHRC: Equality and Human Rights Commission
FFS: For Fuck's Sake
FM: First Minister
FWR: Feminism and Women's Rights
GC: Gender Critical
GRC: Gender Recognition Certificate
GRR: Gender Recognition Reform (Scotland) Bill
HMP: His Majesty's Prison
HQ: Head Quarters
KC: King's Counsel
KS: Kathleen Stock
LGB: Lesbian Gay Bisexual
LGBT: Lesbian Gay Bisexual Transgender
LGBTQ+: Lesbian Gay Bisexual Transgender Queer Plus
M&S: Marks and Spencer
Met: Metropolitan Police
MP: Member of Parliament
MRA: Men's Rights Activist
MSP: Member of the Scottish Parliament
NCAA: The National Collegiate Athletic Association
OP: Original Poster
POT: Pissed Off Trannies
RPW: Recorded Police Warning
RT HON: Right Honourable
ID: Identification (as in self-ID)
Sex Ed: Sex Education
SJB: Sarah Jane Baker
SNP: Scottish National Party
SSSAOR: Single Sex Spaces Are Our Right
T: Trans
TERF: Trans Exclusionary Radical Feminist
TRA: Trans Rights Activist
UCI: Union Cycliste Internationale
UN: United Nations
U of A: University of Aberdeen
WI: Women's Institute
WORIADS: Worthy Of Respect In A Democratic Society
WWW: Women Won't Wheesht
XX: Female Sex chromosomes
XY: Male Sex chromosomes

ADDITIONAL INFORMATION

© Boiledbeetle: LurkingMerkin Poems: No. 1 – No. 12
© Elaine Miller: "Highly offensive"

LOCATIONS

No. 1	Chapter 12	Adopt a merkin today	159
No. 2	Chapter 7	Are you on glue?	96
No. 3	Chapter 11	Be mine	147
No. 4	Chapter 2	Beware	39
No. 5	Chapter 8	Lurking merkins	107
No. 6	Chapter 13	Fame	164
No. 7	Chapter 9	Freewheeling	127
No. 8	Chapter 10	It's got a pocket	134
No. 9	Chapter 4	Holyrood toilets	65
No. 10	Chapter 6	Furry	84
No. 11	Chapter 5	Lurk lurk	78
No. 12	Chapter 15	Lurkers	191
Elaine Miller	Afterword	Highly offensive	205

"Fuck this shit!"

Magdalen Berns

(1983 – 2019)

Printed in Dunstable, United Kingdom